Sometimes It Breaks
Your Heart

Dr. Richard Orzeck

Purrfect Love Publishing
Trumansburg, New York 14886

© 2000 by Dr. Richard Orzeck

Purrfect Love Publishing
PO Box 655
Trumansburg, New York 14886
(607) 387-3490

Printed in the U.S.A.

10 9 8 7 6 5 4 3 2 1

Library of Congress Preassigned Number: 13140

ISBN: 0-9704275-0-6 (perfect bound)
0-9704275-1-4 (case bound)

for Theresa
who lived every single story in this book with me

ACKNOWLEDGMENTS

In the act of bringing this collection of short stories to life, I am deeply indebted to three wonderful people: First, Ms. Rhonda Blaine who, with the patience of a saint, deciphered and transcribed onto computer diskette my nearly illegible doctor's handwriting, transforming it into a workable first draft. Next, Ms. Sandra Su, a true master of the English language, whose proofreading talent and objective suggestions made this chaotic collection of words and thoughts readable. And lastly, Mr. Jeff Burns, a genuine computer wizard, who, with the deftness of a brain surgeon, managed to rescue the various rewrites of this book from the oblivion of cyberspace every time I accidentally hit the wrong button on the computer keyboard.

With all of my heart, I'd like to thank my many treasured clients who, with unwavering trust, have placed the care of their precious pets into my hands.

Finally, to everyone who has ever felt the pain and emptiness; who has ever had to endure the feeling of absolute helplessness; who has ever grieved at the loss of their beloved pet. This book is especially for you.

PREFACE

The following book is a collection of short stories that explore the anguish and heartache of pet loss as seen through the eyes of a country vet. All of the stories are true. Some details and most names have been modified or changed slightly in order to make a point or to protect an identity. The story of Chief and Molly is a composite of two nearly identical cases. The story of Old Ben is, likewise, a combination of various cases that, in one form or another, still occur almost weekly in my practice.

A couple of years back, a client and good friend, Joan, stopped into my office with the express purpose of simply picking up some worm pills. While waiting at the front desk, she just happened to look into my exam room and saw that another client, my wife, and I were in the process of vaccinating a litter of twelve squirmy, seven-week-old basset puppies. With their sad little brown eyes always twinkling innocently and their long ears hanging down to the ground, basset pups are always a precious sight. But this batch that we were working on, were exceptionally adorable.

Anyway, because I was so intent on my examination of these little guys, I don't know for sure just how long she had been standing there; I have the feeling it was quite some time. When at last I finally chanced to look up from the pup I was working on, she looked me in the eye and, smiling the biggest smile you could ever see, she said, "Doc, you have got to have the greatest job in the world."

And she was right. Most of the time, I really, *really,* love this job. But there are moments—fortunately, not too many—that I wish I could just run away and never, ever stop. Times when an owner's good intention turns to tragedy; when an owner's neglect, laziness, or just plain ignorance leads to an innocent animal's death; or the times when all you can do is stand by helplessly, despite all of the many, many miracles of modern medicine, as a newborn little lamb or an infant kitten gasps its last breath. Yes, I agree absolutely with Joan that this is the greatest job in the world. But sometimes, it just breaks your heart.

CONTENTS

CHAPTER ONE

LAMBIE PIE

"Sold," said the auctioneer, "to the young couple in the back." And with the fall of his auction hammer, my wife and I were in the sheep business. We'd just become the proud parents of a beautiful, four-year-old ewe.

Although I was very pleased with myself at the seemingly good deal I'd just made, I kept having this nagging suspicion. Somewhere, way in the back of my mind, a little voice was telling me that the purchase price of seventeen dollars seemed awfully inexpensive for a young, registered, pregnant sheep. But I told myself that it was probably just one of those situations of being in the right place at the right time and, God simply wanted us to have this particular sheep.

We decided to call our new sheep Mama Dorset because, first of all, she was a purebred Dorset sheep and, secondly, in another couple of months, she was going to be a mama. As we were loading her onto our cattle truck, our friend and fellow sheep farmer, Gerald, stopped by to say hello. After a couple of seconds of critically eyeing our new purchase, he said, "That's a fine-looking sheep you got yourself there."

Gerald was one of those wise, old country sages who'd been in the sheep business since the time of Moses, so I was pleased with his assessment. But as I looked down from where I was standing on the back of the truck in order to thank him, I noticed he was still intently studying the sheep. And as he did so, the look of concern on his weathered and ancient face told me that he was grappling with some sort of intense, internal conflict. I didn't know it just then, but he'd seen something wrong with the animal, and he was trying his best to come up with a compassionate way to break the bad news to me.

After what seemed like an eternity, he put it to me straight: "Richard, did ya notice that she only has one tit?"

I looked over to my wife, then back at Gerald, then back to my wife, and then down at Mama Dorset. Before saying a word, I knelt down and reached under Mama Dorset's belly in between her back legs and felt her udder.

"Son of a gun," I mumbled to myself as my hand verified Gerald's discovery.

Sure enough, instead of the two nipples that should have been there, there was only one. Because my wife and I were dairy farmers, we should have known to check the udder of any farm animal before buying it, but somehow, some way, this most basic of observations slipped by us.

Standing up, quite embarrassed and just a little disheartened by it all, I sighed, "No Gerald, I guess I missed it."

There followed several moments of hard silence as we all pondered the situation. Then, after what seemed like another eternity, with a wisdom and grace that can only come from having lived a long and thoughtful life, Gerald decided it would be best at this delicate moment for my wife and me and our new sheep to be left alone. I thanked him sincerely for his revelation, and we all said good-bye.

But as he started to walk away, he paused for a second, turned back around, and said, "Ya know, Richard, having one tit shouldn't affect her none though; she's still a mighty fine-looking sheep."

And he was absolutely right. Having only one teat was not that big a deal. All we would have to do was bottle-feed any lambs that didn't have access to Mama Dorset's single nipple. So we let this one minor flaw just drift from our thoughts. All that mattered now was that we were the proud owners of a beautiful Dorset ewe, that it was a stunningly beautiful September afternoon, and we were as happy as two clams with our purchase.

September soon gave way to October, and as it did, Mama Dorset's belly got bigger and bigger with the lambs that were growing inside her. And then, as expected, come early November, Mama gave birth to twin baby girls. We named the two precious new-born lambs Hot Dog and Lambie Pie. Because she was the biggest and strongest of the pair, Hot Dog got Mama Dorset's single nipple, and Lambie Pie got fed the bottle.

My wife took to bottle-feeding Lambie Pie like she'd been feeding lambs her whole life. Until Lambie Pie was two weeks old, she fed the little lamb every four hours around the clock. To make this task easier, we kept Lambie Pie in a box in our house. Hot Dog and Mama Dorset stayed in a pen down in our dairy cow barn.

What a little joy Lambie Pie was for us. She got so when she wanted her bottle, she'd rustle around in her box and then let out a couple of cute little baby lamb baas to get our attention. After she was fed and rested, she would always want to play. Her favorite trick was to run back and forth around the corner of the living room between the bathroom and kitchen. Sometimes, she'd get moving so fast that she'd bounce along the carpeted floor on all four hooves, just like a gazelle.

She was really quite remarkable. If it was a nice day outside, we'd take her for a walk, and she'd follow us just like a little dog. It was quite a treat to see her hopping and bobbing through the pasture as we walked along.

Because she had to be fed every four hours, we took her and her box with us everywhere we went. If we went to visit the relatives, we'd take Lambie Pie. If we had to travel a couple of hours to get farm machinery parts, we'd take her with us. We even took her along when we went to visit my grandmother in the city, and Lambie Pie behaved like a perfect angel. She'd stay in her box until we took her out, and then she'd run around just like at home.

During this same visit, we made a side trip to visit my aunt and uncle and brought Lambie Pie with us. My cousins and their neighbors absolutely loved her. And even my dear aunt, who never was a farm girl, found her to be just irresistible.

One time, after a particularly long period of bouncing and frolicking, Lambie Pie stopped, squatted, and then peed on my aunt's carpet. My wife and I felt terrible and were afraid my aunt would put her foot down and make us take her out to the car.

But no, she just smiled as she brought out a towel and said, "You know how it is; when you gotta go, you gotta go."

But Lambie Pie kept growing and growing, and by December, she had gotten too big for her box. Also, from our experience with cows and other farm animals, we knew she would have to start eating the same foods as her mother and sister if she was going to grow up normally. So, with great apprehension, we moved her down to the cattle barn and into a nice little box stall we'd made specially for her.

And she didn't mind. The first night, of course, my wife got up a couple of times and went to the barn to check on her. But she was doing just fine. It was like she instinctively knew that was where she belonged. Every morning as we turned on the lights and walked into the barn, she'd get right up, hop up and down, and bleat in her stall to welcome us.

All went just fine until four days before Christmas. As soon as we walked into the barn and turned on the lights, my wife knew something was wrong. Immediately she ran over to her little pen and cried out in horror at what she saw. It was just terrible. Our beautiful little Lambie Pie was dead.

Chapter Two

Lace

It took us a long time to get over our loss of Lambie Pie. A real, real, long time. And what made the tragedy even more devastating was the fact that we couldn't find out with any certainty the reason why she died. Our local vet, who was an excellent cow doctor, offered several suggestions. We talked about Salmonella infections, Clostridia infections, bloat, overeating, and on and on. But there was no one disease we could hang our hat on.

In an effort to try to find out the cause of her death for myself, I began to obsessively read every single book on the subject of veterinary diseases I could lay my hands on. I was, however, at this time, still just an uneducated farmer; to my nonmedical trained mind, very little of what I read made any sense. Besides just trying to satisfy the all-too-human need for the answer as to why little Lambie Pie died, the more important goal for all of this research was to learn how to avoid the problem again. It was critical for us to find the answer, because good old Mama Dorset was pregnant again.

The search for an answer to Lambie Pie's death had one other side effect: All of the reading I was doing absolutely fascinated me, and looking back, it was one of several factors that would eventually lead to my decision to become a veterinarian.

Winter had turned to spring, and spring then turned to summer. We rented a purebred male sheep from our good friend Gerald in order to breed our now gigantic flock of five Dorset ewes. And as expected, come late October, Mama Dorset again blessed us with two beautiful lambs: a boy, who we didn't name, and a little girl, who we called Lace. We named her Lace because she looked so dainty and delicate. The more robust of the two, the boy, ended up getting Mama Dorset's lone nipple. Lacie got the bottle.

This time, we did everything we could to avoid any repeat of the problem we had with Lambie Pie. We made sure she got her colostrum (this is a mother's first milk that helps to protect newborns from disease), and we made sure to sterilize the nursing bottle and artificial nipples. One book, even though it defied logic, suggested only feeding her chilled—versus warmed-up—milk.

And little Lacie did just fine. Not only that, she also worked her little personality into our hearts just like Lambie Pie did. She especially liked it when we picked her up and held her close to our faces because she loved to suck the tips of our noses.

All went along just fine until one cold and blustery early December afternoon. My wife noticed that about an hour after Lacie's noontime bottle feeding, the lamb seemed to be in some discomfort. Her left flank was starting to distend outward, a condition known to farmers as bloat. No problem, I was well read up on the possibility of bloat and was prepared with several remedies. By evening, she was her normal, happy self again, just a-hoppin' and bobbin' around the living room like nothing had ever happened.

The next day, however, she wasn't quite right again. Although she nursed her bottle with great appetite, she seemed to be in a little bit of pain. So, not wanting to take any chances, we took Lacie into our vet's office in town. He examined her, noted that she was very painful when he felt her abdomen and guts, and gave her an injection and some drugs for us to take home. She seemed much better by early that afternoon.

But after a small midafternoon feeding, her belly again started to distend with gas, and she was in a lot of pain. We rushed her back to our vet's office, where we had to anxiously wait an hour for his return from a farm call. He again, very patiently, explained (he was a very kind man) what was going on and then proceeded to stick a needle through the skin on the side of her belly into the air pocket. This procedure worked marvelously to relieve the gas and her pain. When I asked why Lacie was bloating so much, he said he didn't know. As we got ready to leave, he handed me the needles and made sure I knew how to use them.

We went back home to milk the cows. Lacie seemed much better until about eight that night, when she once again started to fill up with gas. And this time she really hurt. Her pain would become so unbearable that she'd flop over on her side, stretch her legs out as far as she could, and cry out in agony.

After several minutes of frantic indecision, I again called our vet. After we talked for a few minutes, discussing what should be done, quite exasperated, he finally said, "Rich, I don't know what's wrong with your lamb, and I don't have the facility to research it. I showed you how to use that needle to tap off the gas in her belly, so be brave and just do it. I'm sorry. There's nothing else I can do." And he hung up.

So, alone now, and not having any other alternatives, my wife and I agonized over what we were gonna do next. I remember the wind howling outside our house and blasting the frozen snow against our plate-glass picture window. I remember how desolate and helpless I thought it all was. I never had to do anything like this before, and I was terrified. Finally, I knelt down beside our suffering little lamb, mustered up all the courage I could, and stuck the big needle into her distended little belly. Much to my relief, it actually worked. Hissssss, went the gas as it passed through the bore of the needle. But even though she felt better from having the pressure relieved from her guts, she looked really bad. Not knowing what to do next to help her, we did nothing, and she fell asleep.

Around ten o'clock, she whimpered out a couple of small little baas like she was hungry, so we got up, and my wife fixed her a bottle. As we waited for my wife to warm the milk, I picked up her limp and tired little body and held her close to my face. And just as she had done a thousand times before, she reached out with her tiny little mouth and weakly sucked the tip of my nose for what would be the last time.

When the bottle was ready, she nursed down maybe an ounce of formula. Seeing she was too weak for any more, my wife laid her back down on her blanket, and she closed her little brown eyes. When my wife got up for her two A.M. feeding, Lacie was gone.

The next morning, after the milking chores were done, we went one more time down to the woods, the same woods she so loved to frolic in during our walks. We dug another hole through the snow-covered, frozen ground and laid her to rest next to Lambie Pie.

Chapter Three

Cooper

As I walked down the long, blacktop sidewalk toward the classrooms on my first day of vet school, I said to myself, "Well Richard, for better or worse, here you are."

I'd just spent four grueling years in college obtaining a bachelor's degree; I'd taken so many entrance examinations and silly aptitude tests that I couldn't even remember them all; I'd filled out scores of forms, veterinary college applications, asked for letters of recommendation, and written personal essays until my fingers hurt. My wife and I sold her beloved dairy herd, our farm, our house, and then packed up all our remaining animals and moved a hundred miles away from family and friends, just so this moment could occur. Despite all of these sacrifices, I felt pretty good because now I was gonna learn all of the answers.

The first week of vet school was spent on orientation. It was during this time that my classmates and I learned just about everything there was to know about one another. We got to know each other's names, our spouse's names, our parents' names, our hobbies, our pets' names, as well as what our goals, dreams, and ambitions were for this chosen profession of ours.

During this week, it was also made clear to us by the staff and faculty of the college, in no uncertain terms, what would be expected of us all, both academically and behaviorally. But the most important outcome of the orientation period was that we would learn how to bond as a class. We would be eighty-one very bright, hard driving, and talented individuals (to this day I have no idea how I made it into this assembly) who would, for the next four years, act and behave as one big, and mostly happy, family.

Then classes started, and the reality of our situation hit us like a sledgehammer. This was serious stuff we needed to learn, and there would be no time for fooling around: anatomy, physiology, endocrinology, histology, pathology, pharmacology, plus many, many, more courses too numerous to mention. Stuffed in between all of these lectures were all-afternoon laboratories, clinical rounds with the doctors, guest speakers, and late-into-the-evening group study sessions.

But of all the courses we had to endure that first year, the most demanding, the most time consuming, and the most interesting was anatomy. It was a well-known fact that if you were the spouse or a friend of a first-year student and you needed to find that person, if you went to the anatomy laboratory, there would be an excellent chance of finding him or her there studying.

In the anatomy lab, we would, either individually or in small groups, spend days at a time examining and studying our personal cadavers, laboratory manuals, or one of the many professionally prepared specimens the professors would make available for our use. We would spend hours tracing out and finding for the first time a critical blood vessel or an elusive nerve fiber.

It was demanding work that required a huge amount of time and patience to master. Frequently, one or more of my classmates would bring their dogs along to keep them company.

One of the more popular dogs in my class was a young yellow Labrador named Cooper, who was owned by my good friend and classmate Paul. The two of them were absolutely inseparable; everywhere Paul was, you'd find Cooper. About the only time you didn't see the dog was during the classroom lectures themselves, because pets weren't allowed.

Late one night, about one month into our fall classes, a large group of us were in the anatomy lab intently studying our specimens in preparation for our first anatomy exam. Cooper, as always, was at Paul's feet contentedly gnawing on a large rawhide bone.

All of a sudden, the dog jumped up, stretched out his neck as far as he could, and started gagging and hacking and wouldn't stop. Apparently, he had broken loose a chunk of the rawhide bone, and it had become stuck somewhere in his throat.

Although it was a scary problem, the thought occurred to us that there was no better place to be with a dog with a chunk of leather stuck in his windpipe than at one of the greatest vet schools in the world. At the time, the problem didn't seem all that bad because he could still walk around and breathe just fine. Paul and a couple of other classmates took Cooper over to the hospital's emergency room and I, since it was quite late, went home.

The next morning, when I walked into the lecture hall, I knew immediately that something was wrong. The lecture room, normally abuzz with gossip and chatter, was real quiet, and any conversations that were going on were subdued.

Sitting down next to my friend Steve, I asked him what was going on. He said that Paul's dog Cooper had died last night during his emergency surgery.

I was positively stunned. "Gosh, he didn't seem all that bad," I said.

Steve then went on to tell me that what he'd heard, was that even though the chunk of chew toy wasn't blocking the windpipe completely, it nonetheless still had to be taken out. The only way to remove it was to stick an endoscope (a camera device with a grasping mechanism on its end) down the dog's throat and grab it.

Since no self-respecting dog would allow that to happen while he was awake, the surgeons had to anesthetize him. Although nobody knew for sure at the time—or for that matter, would ever know—what probably happened was that Cooper had a reaction to the anesthetic and his heart stopped.

The effect on our beloved classmate Paul was obvious. We heard he found a place to bury his beloved friend and was out of classes for a couple of days. We all signed a sympathy card and got back to our studies. Paul soon came back around and eventually got another Lab, and we all got on with the serious business of learning to save lives.

But the experience left me—and probably all of my classmates as well—with this great apprehension (another word could be fear) for the use of anesthesia. And for me personally, my hopes for all the answers were totally smashed to pieces; all of my wishes to know what to do were now beyond any hope of redemption. If such a senseless tragedy could happen here at this great university, with the best that veterinary medical science had to offer, then what possible chance would we have as private practitioners when we finally struck out on our own? This revelation that there were still going to be times when I wasn't going to be able to save every animal's life bothered me for a long time. I would learn many wonderful things during my vet school days but, sadly, death was still going to be a frequent companion.

Chapter Four

Buddy

The Labrador on the exam room table in front of me was dying right before my very eyes. In the room with me were Buddy's owners, three sisters, all crying uncontrollably and pleading with me over and over again, "Doctor, we didn't know; we just didn't know. We were only trying to help him. Doctor, please save him. We don't know what we'd do without our Buddy."

I looked up from the limp body of their beloved pet and softly said, "Ladies, Buddy is very sick, but we'll do all we can."

I also reminded them, for the third time, that I wasn't quite a doctor yet, only a forth-year student.

The oldest of the sisters looked at me, wiped her eyes, and as she attempted a smile, said, "That's OK, Doctor, we trust you."

And so began the very first clinical case of my veterinary career.

The case started out simply enough. In veterinary school, when you're a forth-year student doing your first clinical rotations in the hospital, you're considered low man on the totem pole. Your job is to greet the owners, get the patient's history, do the initial physical exam, and then summarize your findings to the intern in charge. The intern then does the same thing all over again. He in turn reports to the on-duty resident, who reports to the professor/doctor. It's a real pain, but that's how we learn.

The professor in charge of determining which incoming patient goes to which student on this particular rotation said to me, "Rich, we've got this really big problem I'd like for you to take care of." It turned out he was right in both the medical and physical sense.

Buddy was an extremely overweight—about 155 pounds—yellow Labrador who was owned by the three elderly maiden sisters now sitting with me in the exam room. Their local vet referred the dog to our university medical center because he was showing signs of potentially fatal liver disease. The doctor knew that Buddy was these ladies' whole life; therefore, if the dog could be saved at all, my university would be the place to do it.

As I continued with my examination of Buddy, the sad truth regarding the cause of his failing liver was revealed. It turned out that the sisters had brought the dog to their local vet because he was having trouble getting up and down and seemed in pain every time he walked. Quite correctly, the vet diagnosed Buddy's problem as severe hip dysplasia. He explained to them the problem was a lot like having bad arthritis and that it was partially the result of his genetics and also the fact that the animal was seventy pounds overweight.

He'd suggested they made sure Buddy took it easy from now on, and if they wanted to ease his pain, they could give him a couple of plain aspirins once or twice a day.

After leaving their vet's office, they went to their local drugstore, searched the shelves, and bought the strongest extra-strength pain reliever they could find. They wanted to do the very best they possibly could for their treasured pet. What they didn't know or check carefully enough was that the product they bought contained not a single grain of aspirin. It was comprised one hundred percent of another very common type of painkiller.

This product, which works like a miracle in humans, is deadly when given to dogs. The bottom line was, they not only ended up giving Buddy a dangerous drug, they were giving it to him in an extra-strength dose. About three days after the sisters began giving him these capsules, Buddy stopped eating. By the next day, he was turning yellow with jaundice, was flat out, and could not get up.

My veterinary training taught me there was going to be very little that I or my great university could do about this disease. It was too late for any antidote, and liver transplants weren't done in dogs at that time.

After finishing my examination, I left the sisters with Buddy while I consulted with the higher-ups on the chain of command. They all confirmed my diagnosis and conclusion and then made some recommendations for treatment. The doctor felt that if we could keep the dog alive long enough, the liver might just regenerate and he would live. However, the chances of this happening were very slim.

After our conference was finished, I had hoped that one of my senior colleagues would do the honor of telling the sisters the results of our discussion. But this was not going to be the case.

"No," they said, "you're gonna have to do it sometime, Richard; now is as good a time as any to start."

I didn't want to go back into that room with the sisters in the worst way. I just felt like running away. But I didn't. I collected my thoughts, got myself calmed down, and with the professor behind me, walked back into the exam room. As the professor stood quietly in the corner, I told the sisters the whole truth, what had happened and why, and gave them our objective opinion on the most likely out-come of Buddy's problem.

The sisters hung onto every word that came out of my mouth like it would be the last words they would ever hear. And without them having to say a word, I knew instantly it wasn't going to go well. Their glassy eyes and blank, silent expressions were all I needed to see that the sisters were devastated by my report.

As their realization of the serious nature of Buddy's disease sank in, and as their guilt got the best of them, they lost all self-control.

"Doctor," they all cried, "please, you gotta do something. Please, you gotta save our baby."

My professor, seeing that the situation might be getting out of hand, then stepped in. In a profes-sional and very calm, detached manner, he restated all of the details of Buddy's poor prognosis.

To the surprise of both of us, the sisters bluntly brushed him aside and said in no uncertain terms, in almost perfect harmony, "Sir, we want him"—pointing to me—"to try any and everything he can to save our Buddy. We trust him."

So, without having the slightest idea of what I was going to do, I assured them I would do my best.

After the ladies left, we all—the professor, resi-dents, interns, and six of my classmates—got together for another conference and worked up a plan for Buddy's hospitalization. There wasn't too much we could do for the poor creature except just keep him going. Another colleague and I placed an intravenous catheter into his nearly lifeless forearm, started him on a fluid drip, gave him an antibiotic injection, and got him set up in a huge floor-level cage in the hospital's intensive care ward. The intensive care nurses then monitored him round the clock while I took care of other patients.

The sisters settled into a downtown motel and prepared themselves to stay for as long as it was going to take. Every morning I would examine Buddy, take blood samples, and give him his antibiotics. Then, promptly at one o'clock sharp, a classmate and I would carry him on a stretcher out to the waiting room, where the sisters would love him and hug him and ask me a million and one questions. Occasionally, when there was a question I couldn't answer, I'd offer to get the professor.

One or another of the ladies would always reply, "Nah, that's OK, Doc. If you don't know the answer, he probably don't either." They were very kind to me.

After their visits, I'd ask the professor their questions anyway, because I didn't want to overlook anything that might benefit Buddy's care. I'd also apologize for the way the sisters were ignoring him.

He'd just laugh and say to me, "Richard, they're comfortable with you, and that's the most important part."

He was a wonderful humanitarian and a good man. Looking back, however, I wonder if there may have been another reason he was glad to avoid the sisters. Besides their dedication to the mission of restoring Buddy's health, it seems they had come to the conclusion that I, or anyone in my close proximity, wasn't getting enough to eat.

Starting with the first visit, there came cookies, pastries, meatball sandwiches, pizzas, and on and on. My professor was glad to have skipped the feeding frenzy; I guess he wanted to maintain his boyish figure.

After three days in intensive care, Buddy actually got a little better. The intravenous fluids I was giving him replaced a lot of his body's much-needed electrolytes, and the glucose gave him a little energy. He got so he could even walk with some assistance.

On the forth day of his stay, during his owners' afternoon visit, the sisters told me of their disappointment in not being able to visit Buddy at times other than the one-hour afternoon visit. I told them it was the hospital's policy, and there was no way around it. However, since Buddy could now walk some, I told the ladies that I would try—but I couldn't guarantee—to arrange my schedule of patients so that I'd have a few minutes to bring him outside for a walk every evening at six.

If they just happened to be driving by at that time, I could probably hang around a couple of minutes more.

They were so elated to hear this good news that each in her own turn hugged me so hard I thought my ribs would break. And so it was that Buddy was the only patient in the hospital who got to see his owners twice a day. For the next three or four days, I found this evening diversion from my grinding schedule of seeing patients, filling out paperwork, and studying for exams a very welcome relief. But as time went on, I could see the worried looks of the sisters getting more and more profound.

Although the patient was looking a little better as time went on, the sisters intuitively knew he was still failing. And they knew they were losing him because, in spite of bringing him daily all of the sausages, pizza crusts, cat food, or other goodies he'd always loved, they simply could not get the poor dog to eat.

Their suspicions were confirmed by Buddy's daily blood tests. Despite the slight boost he was getting from his intravenous fluids, all of his body organs, including his destroyed liver, were beginning to shut down. After about the fifth day of our evening interludes in the parking lot, Buddy got so weak he could no longer walk.

On the last day, during our afternoon visit, my classmate and I carried Buddy into the exam room for the last time. He was so weak he could no longer even lift his head. Because I'd expected the worst with regards to the emotional reactions from the sisters, I was surprised at what actually happened.

A calm and peaceful composure had come over the ladies that I did not expect. They knew that Buddy had fought the good fight but that now he was tired. The oldest sister, looking to me as she had for the past week, asked, "He's dying, isn't he?"

I slowly nodded yes.

"Then I think it's time, Doctor, that we let him go."

I nodded again in sincere agreement with their decision and called the on-duty resident into the room. (I couldn't legally give the euthanasia shot myself yet.) Then, after each sister said farewell to their cherished friend, Buddy closed his eyes for the last time.

CHAPTER FIVE

BABE

The long, heartbreaking struggle was finally over; old Babe the elephant was dead. For the past several weeks, the greatest veterinary minds in the world had given their all to try to save this gentle creature, but in the end, her sickness proved to be just too much for her to bear.

Babe's death—and that of her stillborn infant—was a terrible loss, not only for the community who knew and loved her but for all of the elephant kingdom as well. Likewise, the controversy concerning the many decisions that led up to this devastating end would go on and on and on. But for now, all anyone knew for certain was that this beautiful animal, who never harmed a soul in her whole life, was gone; for now, it was all over but the crying. And her autopsy.

It was because of Babe's autopsy that I came to be standing on a loading dock outside of my vet school's pathology department in a cold, drizzling rain, watching the workmen from our local electric company as they unloaded the elephant's giant body from the back of a huge crane truck.

I was about to become part of a team of about 150 students, pathologists, and scientists who were going to perform the first-ever complete autopsy of an Asian elephant.

As we all stood there watching and waiting for the workmen to complete their sorrowful task, we talked among ourselves and shared what details we may have known about Babe's illness and the tragic series of events that had led up to her death.

From what we could gather, the decision to breed Babe had been made with the noblest intentions. It's a sad fact that because of the destruction of their habitat and the encroachment of man into the creature's native environment, the Asian elephant is facing the real possibility of extinction in the wild within the next quarter of a century.

And so, in order to try to delay this most un-thinkable of events from occurring, zoos and wildlife parks throughout the world are participating in well-organized captive breeding programs in an effort to increase the overall numbers of these elephants.

We also learned that this decision was not made without some controversy. Babe, who'd never had a baby in her twenty-six years of life, seemed an almost perfect candidate for participation in this breeding program. She was gentle and sociable and in perfect health. But some considered her to be a little old to become a first-time mother. Finally, after weighing all of the pros and cons, the judgment was made by her vet to go ahead and try to get her pregnant. Within a short time, a fine-looking male was located and brought to the zoo. And before you knew it, sweet old Babe was with child.

What an exciting time it was for everyone involved! This was going to be the first time an Asian elephant had ever given birth at the zoo, and everyone went all out for the occasion. The enthusiasm of the community to be part of this landmark event was overwhelming. There was everything from name-the-baby contests to throwing Babe an old-fashioned bridal shower. It was all going along just perfectly; too perfectly, as time would later prove.

This is where the information my classmates and I were sharing on that rainy, cold loading dock became a little less clear. The best we all could figure out was that as Babe's due date got closer and closer, her veterinarian became concerned that she just wasn't acting the way an elephant who's about to give birth should act.

So she called in a team of reproductive experts (veterinary pediatricians) from my university. After examining Babe and consulting with other specialists from all over the world, they determined that the infant elephant still in her womb was dead. Even worse, the dead baby was starting to decay, and it was making Babe sick.

Her veterinarian was then stuck with two terrible choices. The first was to just wait and see if the antibiotics and other drugs Babe had been given would keep her alive long enough for her to pass the dead fetus on her own. The other option was to do a C-section, that is, to remove the dead baby surgically. Because doing a C-section on an Asian elephant had never been done successfully, the decision was made to wait.

Several days passed and nothing happened, except that poor old Babe just got sicker and sicker. She just seemed to have lost the desire to go on. And so, after waiting as long as they dared, her caregivers made the difficult decision to perform a C-section.

The details involved in trying to surgically remove a several-hundred-pound infant from the belly of a several-thousand-pound elephant were just about beyond comprehension. But somehow, after several hours of backbreaking work, the doctors managed to open up Babe's belly, get the baby out, and then successfully sew her back up. All of the surgeons involved seemed to feel that the operation went fairly well.

For a while, it seemed as if Babe just might recover. She would walk around some with her vet and handlers, and for a short period of time she even seemed to enjoy playing with her favorite car tire toy. But it didn't last long; Babe had lost her will to live.

And so, on the morning of her last day, her veterinarian removed all of her life support tubes from her gigantic body and thus let her die with dignity. The pathologist would state her cause of death as due to complications of pregnancy. But people who were with her during her last days all knew she died of a broken heart.

But Babe's death would not be in vain. An enormous amount of information was learned and documented during her pregnancy and subsequent death. Even more important, for the first time in history, an Asian elephant was going to get a proper autopsy. The only place this could ever be done properly, because of the sheer amount of manpower and facilities needed, was at a university. And that's how Babe saw fit to include me in this episode.

To a person with little or no medical training, the idea of autopsying poor old Babe might seem ghoulish. I read it in the newspapers and heard it with my own ears: "Oh, those heartless scientists and doctors, they just couldn't wait for her to die so they could perform experiments on her. How could they do such a terrible thing?"

But as I mentioned above, the Asian elephant is on the verge of extinction. Because of this, it's important for medical science to learn all it can whenever it can. Ultimately, what we learned from the scientists' work on Babe would fill volumes. Tissue samples from her would be sent to researchers all over the world: to gastrointestinal experts in France, to a neurologist in Sweden studying nerve function in the elephant trunk, to reproductive physiologists in India, and to numerous other specialist all over the world. The bottom line is that autopsying is the only way we can learn what we need to know about this majestic creature.

After Babe was unloaded and properly positioned for her autopsy, I took my assigned place between the front legs near her head. My job was to begin removing her skin, which would prepare the way for another team to start the difficult task of dismantling her front leg.

As we all stood there in the now-pouring rain waiting for the word to start, a small pickup truck pulled up alongside Babe's giant body. While we all watched, a lady got out of the truck and walked slowly over to near where I was standing. Seemingly unaware of all of us, she knelt down hard on the wet blacktop next to Babe's head and started to weep.

Someone later told me he thought she was Babe's vet. Someone else told me no, it wasn't her vet, it was her handler. But it really didn't matter. Without knowing so at the time, I was witnessing firsthand a scene that has taken place for all of the thousands of years man and animals have walked our earth side by side: the solemn last moments between the doctor and her patient, a caregiver and her dependent, or the cherished life companion and her now-departed friend.

Whoever she was, we who watched her knew immediately that she and Babe had shared a long, hard struggle together, but it was now time to say the final good-bye. After several minutes of lovingly caressing gentle old Babe's peaceful face, she leaned forward, kissed the elephant above its beautiful little eye, turned her lips down to just in front of the animal's giant ear, and silently whispered her private farewell. She gently pulled a couple of whiskers from Babe's chin for a keepsake; then she stood up and, without looking back or saying a single word, she walked to her pickup, got in, and drove away. Her journey with Babe was now complete.

For us on the autopsy team, however, the long night was just beginning. We all had mixed emotions about what we were preparing to do. We were sorrowful at the loss of this noble creature and deeply touched at the poignant scene we'd all just witnessed. But there was also a sense of adventure about the journey of discovery we were preparing to embark on. We all knew that this was more than just important, it was almost sacred. We were determined to ensure that Babe's death would not be in vain.

When the order to start was finally given, I crouched down between Babe's front legs, autopsy knife in hand and ready to go. But as I scooched my body around in an attempt to find a comfortable working position, I happened to turn and look down in the direction of my left elbow. Just as I did, I was squirted in the face by an unknown liquid. Surprised—and just a little frightened—I scrambled back up to my feet to find out what in the world had happened.

Looking down, I discovered that my elbow had accidentally pressed against one of Babe's breasts, and what I'd been squirted with was her milk; the life-giving milk that she never had the chance to share with her stillborn little baby.

As I stood there with the precious liquid running down my face, I thought one last time about Babe lying there, the milk still dripping from her breast getting washed indifferently away by the cold April rain. I thought about her dear, deceased baby and what an amazing little creature he would have been. I thought about the lady who just minutes before had graced all of us with her dignified and heartfelt good-bye to a friend.

But the spell was broken by the professor in charge who asked me, in his usual blunt manner, "Orzeck, you gonna stand there all night with your head up your butt (butt wasn't exactly the word he used) or are you going to join the rest of the group and get to work?"

Without saying a word, I wiped the rain and milk from my face with my bare left arm, squatted back down, and got to cutting.

CHAPTER SIX

POODLES

Sometimes I just don't understand some people. Maybe it's just me, but the way I see it, we mortal human beings have just one chance at this life and that's it; just one shot to be alive and live on this beautiful—this stunningly beautiful—planet.

Most people I come into contact with do so just fine. There are, however, the occasional individuals that I'll meet or read about in the newspaper who, despite being in both good physical and mental health, seem to be doing everything they possibly can to let this precious, God-given opportunity pass them by.

We hear about these poor souls all of the time. Spiteful, mean, selfish individuals who, for reasons known only to them, live their desperate lives and then die. There's the eccentric old bachelor who dies alone in some old shack out by the railroad tracks who had nearly every dollar he'd ever made in his life stuffed into banana boxes under his bed. Or the old spinster living in her run-down Victorian mansion, alone and afraid, her windows frozen shut from never having been opened in fifty years.

Just after graduating from vet school and just prior to starting my own practice, I worked at a four-doctor clinic in beautiful upstate New York. I could not have found a better place anywhere in which to begin my life as a new veterinarian. I was treated with respect, paid well, and if I had a problem I couldn't handle, was generously given any assistance I may have needed. However, because I was the low man on the totem pole, I was on call for a lot of weekend work. And most of the time I was on my own.

Around nine o'clock on one of these Saturday mornings, Dorothy, one of the clinic's veterinary technicians, brought a pet carrier into the treatment room where I was tending to a hospitalized patient and placed it on one of the exam tables. Although normally a jolly and upbeat sort of person, I could tell by her troubled expression that she was upset about something. When I asked what was wrong, she didn't answer; she just stood there, looking into the cage.

So I finished quickly what I was doing, walked over to the table where she had just set the pet carrier down, and took a look inside.

There were two of the most adorable little toy poodles you would ever want to see. One was black and the other was an apricot. Both just stood there panting, with their little pink tongues hanging out, as happy as could be, just wagging away with their stubby little tails.

Thinking to myself they were probably just here for a simple heartworm test or something like that, I sort of laughed and said to Dorothy, "They look pretty good to me, what are we doing with these guys?"

It took a couple of seconds for Dorothy to collect herself. Whatever it was we were going to have to do, I could tell it was killing her. "They're here for you to put to sleep."

And then she left the room. I think she was crying. For a second, I just stood there, absolutely stunned. I thought to myself, "What possible reason could there be for anybody to want to euthanize these two young and obviously healthy dogs? Especially two poodles?"

I knew for a fact that I could adopt them out in a heartbeat. And so, before doing anything else, I went to front desk of the hospital's waiting room and asked receptionist what the story was with these two dogs.

She, likewise, was upset by the whole situation. It turned out that a lawyer had brought the dogs into the clinic to fulfill a last request of an elderly lady client of his law firm who had, just a couple of days ago, passed away. For reasons known only to her, she had stipulated in her will that upon her death, the law firm was to have these two young poodles put to sleep and their remains then buried in her backyard.

The lawyer said his client's instructions were perfectly clear on the matter. Additionally, in the cold, objective manner for which many members of his profession are famous, he said he himself would return just before the clinic's noontime closing and retrieve the remains. He said that he needed to insure the lady's wishes were carried out. And that was that.

Since I was the only doctor on duty that weekend morning, the macabre task would have to fall on my shoulders. I went back into the treatment room where the two little dogs were still anxiously waiting without a care in the world other than wondering why they had to stay in their cage. I sat down and thought about what I was going to do. I still had a couple of hours to try to figure out a way around all this grief. I didn't want to do this job in the worst way, and so I just put it off.

As I went about finishing the remainder of the morning's hospital rounds and treatments, I thought back to just a few years before and remembered my first experience with euthanasia of what I thought was a healthy animal. I was in my last year of vet school and doing an externship at a huge veterinary clinic in Boston. It was about eight o'clock in the morning, and the doctor I was assigned to asked me to meet him in the hospital's kennel room. He arrived about five minutes later with a syringe full of a deep blue liquid. He asked me to retrieve this absolutely gorgeous German shepherd from the kennel, making sure that I muzzle her, and then bring her to the treatment room.

I said OK and walked over to the wall where the leather muzzles and nylon leads were hanging and grabbed one of each. I then walked up to the kennel door, let her smell my hand some to make sure she was friendly (she was), and then opened the door.

She came running right to me and pranced around the room just wanting to be played with and petted. I then got a leash around her neck and we walked into the treatment room together. As we entered the room, the doctor, for no good reason that I could tell, shouted, "Richard, damn it all! I told you to put a muzzle on that dog; do it now!"

I was a little startled by his sudden change of attitude because, up until this moment, even though I felt he had quite an exaggerated opinion of himself, he hadn't been, in any way, all that bad a guy.

I paused for a second, and then looked him squarely in the eye; I wanted real badly to tell him to take the darn muzzle and put it where the sun don't shine, but I didn't dare; I still had to depend upon this little creep's evaluation of my performance. Although I didn't say anything, I held his gaze.

After what seemed like hours, he realized he was dealing with someone who wasn't going to take any of his abuse, and so he dropped his eyes and cowered away some. After a couple more seconds, I did what he said.

I had no idea what was going on. When we finally got the dog around into the good light, he asked me to hold off the vein. No big deal, I thought. It looked like all we were just going to do was put the dog under anesthesia for some minor procedure such spaying or dentistry. And so I straddled the dog, reached down, and squeezed my hand around her left leg, just above the elbow, in order to raise up the vein. I was shocked by what happened next.

The doctor kneeled down in front of the dog, placed the needle into the dog's vein, and the injected the contents of the syringe. In about a second, the dog collapsed; and in another couple of seconds she was dead.

"Doctor, what did you just do?" I demanded.

The little wise guy stood up with a vicious smirk and said, "Come on Richard, you're almost a doctor, what's the heck does it look like?"

Doing my best to contain my anger, I calmly asked, "Doctor, I can see she's dead, but why in the world did you do it?"

Obviously annoyed by my impertinence (I was, after all, just a lowly student, and a visiting student at that), but a little bit nervous because he knew that if he bullied me too far, I could crush him like the little worm he was, he answered, "The dog had bitten a visiting nephew, and so the owner had her destroyed."

As I stood there next to the limp mass of fur, he added, "Leave her there. The cage cleaning staff will take care of her. We gotta get cleaned up and start our morning rounds."

It took me a long time to get over that morning. Later that day, as I was discussing the morning's events with the hospital supervisor, I mentioned the doctor's arrogant behavior toward me. She just kind of laughed to herself and told me something that even to this day I've never forgotten. She said that he always acted like that when he had to do something he didn't want to do.

"He didn't want to put that poor dog to sleep any more than you did. He acted like a moron because that's his way of dealing with it. We do what we have to do, and someday, Richard, you'll be in his shoes."

Indeed, there I was. I thought about the lady who had owned the poodles and wondered what kind of selfish, spiteful, miserable person she must have been. There might have been some logic in the whole thing if the dogs were old or infirm. Then it would have been a kind choice. But this wasn't the case. These were young dogs. I think that she felt that if she couldn't have them, then no one could.

I wish that I could put into words the paralyzing tug-of-war of thoughts that were going on in my mind as the noon hour approached. I really didn't want to do this, and I fought it right up until the last moment. The small Saturday morning staff all knew the burden I was carrying and were very respectful and patient with my procrastination.

But as the clock read quarter to twelve, the vet tech firmly said, "Doctor, the lawyer is going to be here any minute, and it's time for us all to go home. Come on, Doc, let's get it over with."

I nodded. As she gently pulled the first dog (the apricot one) out of the cage, I walked over to the cabinet and got the euthanasia solution and a syringe. As I drew the required amount of solution up into the syringe, she lovingly held off the vein on the dog's front leg. I gritted my teeth, cleared my mind of all thoughts and feeling, placed the needle into the vein, and emptied the syringe.

Without a single word spoken, the tech got the other dog out of the cage as I filled the syringe again. I gritted my teeth one last time and finished the job.

As the tech went to get a couple of plastic bags, I stood there looking down on the now-lifeless bodies lying side by side on the table in front of me. I'd like to say that I felt anguish for the poor little creatures, or maybe sorrow for their loss, but I didn't, at least not at first. My heart was so broken that I didn't feel anything. I just stood there trying to figure out what in the heck just happened.

But as the seconds ticked by, my numbness changed into anger. The anger grew into rage. I thought of these little guys' owner over and over again and wondered what possible motivation could have compelled her to pass such a heartless and selfish judgment upon them. What were the demons lurking in her mind?

As the tech returned and she and the staff began carefully bagging up the little poodles' remains for the lawyer now waiting out front, I half shouted, half growled, "I gotta get out of here, see you all on Monday."

I slammed the door as I left.

Chapter Seven

Suzie

People are always asking me why I decided to be a veterinarian instead of becoming a *"real doctor."* When this happens, the first thing I do is try to stay calm, take a deep breath, and no matter what, just smile as big a smile as I can. I make it a point to resist the temptation to answer their insensitivity with the lame statement, "Sir (or ma'am), but I am a real doctor," because it would only embarrass both of us.

Instead, I jokingly tell them that even though I love my fellow humans a lot, they can be a real pain in the neck when they're sick and that I just didn't want to have to listen to their endless whining and complaining all of the time. (One exception to this is, of course, myself. My wife tells me I'm a perfect angel when I'm ill.)

Actually, when I think about it in moments of quiet reflection, there are really only two things I envy with regards to my human doctor colleagues: The first is that physicians are able to have nice carpeting and furniture in their waiting rooms. This would not work at all in my veterinary office. I could almost guarantee you that the first dog into my clinic the day after the carpet was installed would be a one-hundred-sixty-pound, intact rottweiler who would insist on watering down every chair leg and corner in the room.

The second, and by far the more serious, is that human doctors are not allowed to practice euthanasia. That is, human doctors can't—at least not yet—put their patients to sleep like we vets can. If you really think about it, the ability to end an animal's suffering with something as simple as an injection is an awesome responsibility.

And mostly, in cases of severe suffering and debilitating injuries, I'm thankful I have this gift as an option. There are times, however, I wish I just didn't have to deal with it.

Our Suzie was a very special cat. I first met her when I was just a young and angry ex-sailor home from the Vietnam War, doing my best to try to make a living milking cows. My girlfriend—who's now my wife, Theresa—had originally found the cat in a dairy barn where she had been working the summer before. When she'd first found her, Suzie was just a scraggly little kitten, the daughter of a wild and untouchable mother cat. She was a black and gray short-haired tabby cat with a big white patch on her muzzle as well as white socks on all four feet. She was a petite cat who never weighed more that five pounds. When Theresa and I got married, Suzie came with the deal (as did my very-much-loved in-laws).

As I look back to those hard and endless days on the dairy farm, I realize now that it was because of Suzie that I became a true cat lover. It's not that I actually hated cats prior to meeting her, I was just indifferent to their presence. Although my wife was her most-favorite person in the world, right from the start Suzie did what she could to become my friend. She would walk by and give me an opportunity to pet her or pick her up, but I didn't give her a second glance.

But no matter how hard I tried to do so, Suzie would not let me ignore her. As I sat in my chair in the barn having a coffee break or trying to do some book work, she would insist on rubbing up against my legs, wanting both my attention and affection. If I didn't respond, she'd jump up onto the table next to the chair and just sit there, silently tilting her head to one side or the other, as she gazed at me with her eager little eyes.

Every morning as we did the chores, she would alternate her attention between my wife, who did the milking, and I, who did the feeding. Suzie liked being on the barn floor the most during milking time because my wife would frequently put a few splashes of warm, fresh milk into her kitty dish. When she had her fill of milk, she would amble over and lie on the windowsill, contently watching me as I fed the cows. After the milking chores were done, she would head to the milk house and help my wife as she cleaned the milking equipment. Suzie especially liked getting the excess milk from the bottom of the milking pails. When finished here, she would meander back out into the barn and keep me company as I cleaned and bedded down the cows.

After I was accepted to vet school, we retired from the dairy business and moved off the farm. Suzie, without a bit of difficulty, readily made the transition from barn cat to house cat. Although she preferred being outside at night, it didn't take her long to discover that if she sat on the railing by the back patio doors, I would let her in when I awoke early in the morning and was making my coffee.

She knew that after pouring my first cup, I'd walk over to the refrigerator for the quart of milk, at which time she'd just sit by her kitty dish, silently reminding me to not forget to pour her a small splash of milk as well.

Then, as I sat at my library desk writing a term paper for class, studying my brains out for an upcoming test, or just plain enjoying my morning coffee, she would always be there beside me, sitting on the armrest of the sofa, purring me onward. After finishing my first cup, she would patiently sit by the kitty dish as I poured a second one, silently waiting for me to give her another small taste of milk. Finally, as I sat at the table putting my shoes on and getting ready to walk out the door to school, she would perform this little dance on the kitchen floor until I gave her a few Pounce kitty treats.

When at last I graduated from vet school and started my new practice in the garage of my house, Suzie (and all of our other cats) was there beside me to help me greet my new clients. She would always sit on the far corner of my big wooden physician's desk—where, I'm sure, she felt she was safe from the many canine patients—and examine, with that curious way she had, all of the pet owners.

As my practice grew and I had to move to an office in town, she resumed the role of being just a plain family cat. She still insisted, however, on being let inside every morning when I made my coffee.

It didn't matter whether it was five o'clock or seven o'clock in the morning, she'd always be out there on the back patio railing waiting for me. And, like before, it didn't matter at all what I was doing at my desk. Whether I was reading medical journal articles or writing my newspaper column, she was faithfully there on the arm of the chair next to my desk, watching me in that cute little way she had, making sure I did everything correctly.

But, as millions of pet owners in the world all know, one of the more poignant aspects of having a dear pet is that we have to watch them grow old in what always seems too short a time. Our hearts soar with joy—an occasional frustration—as we watch them run and jump and scurry everywhere with the boundless energy that is symbolic of their youth.

As they mature and reach the stability of middle age, we delight in their companionship; we are comforted by their nearness to us; and we are touched by their absolute and non-judgmental love. And then all too soon, just as we really get to know them, just when they have firmly worked their way into our hearts, they're taken from us.

I still remember, even after all of this time—like it was yesterday—the hot August morning I had to put our Suzie to sleep. For the better part of her last six months, Suzie's vision had been getting worse and worse until one early summer morning, she showed up on our back patio deck almost completely blind.

Then, a short time later, she somehow hurt her hip and began to have serious trouble walking. Because we were worried for her safety, we kept her caged up when we weren't around.

But Suzie had always been a free spirit from the day she was born, and locking her up in a cage, even if it was for her own good, was grieving her more than her bodily injuries ever would. My wife pointed this out to me daily, and in my heart, I knew she was right. I also knew I could end her suffering in a minute, but I just couldn't bring myself to do it.

Maybe it was wishful thinking; I'd seen some pretty impressive patient recoveries over the years.

Maybe it was just plain cowardice. Maybe I just didn't want to let her go.

As I agonized over what I was soon gonna have to do, my thoughts drifted back to the time a few years before when I'd accidentally backed my car over our young, orange tabby cat, Foobtube, as I was leaving early one morning for vet school. I knew I'd broken the poor guy's back, and there would be little I could do.

At school, I got one of my professors to examine him; he agreed with my diagnosis and offered to put the cat to sleep for me. Like all of my teachers at vet school, he was a very kind man. He said to me, "Richard, you should never have to put one of your own animals to sleep."

Another time, during my last year of classes, our old German shepherd, Brut, had gotten so feeble he could no longer walk. My wife and I, not wanting to let him go, had carried him outside at least five times a day for several months so he could enjoy the beautiful weather and go to the bathroom. As the summer turned into a very cold and rainy autumn, we knew we were going to have to do something with our old friend, but we had neither the resources nor the courage to put him down.

One day in school, one of my classmates and I were talking about my dilemma, and he volunteered to take care of Brut for me. And, God bless him, he got hold of some euthanasia solution (I don't know how, we weren't allowed access to the drug as students), drove out to my farm, and while I held my old dog in my arms, he gave the injection.

With Suzie, however, none of these options were possible. So, not knowing exactly how to deal with the situation, my wife and I just followed the same advice that I routinely give my clients when they ask me how to tell when it is time to put their pets to sleep: "Just watch your pet closely, and they'll tell you when they're ready."

And so time went on, and it took a little getting used to, but I finally stopped looking out the back patio door for Suzie as I walked through the kitchen to my coffeepot. Instead, I would put the coffee perking and then walk out to her cage in my garage and bring her inside. As I poured my first cup, she would patiently look at me with her now crusted-up, blind eyes as if nothing was wrong, just making sure she got her splash of milk.

I would then carry her into my library, and she would sit there on the arm of her chair, just purring and watching me while I worked. Then we would go through the whole routine again of getting a little more milk as I poured my second cup of coffee. She even insisted on getting a couple of Pounce kitty treats as I got ready to head out to the office.

But the quart of milk finally was empty and the Pounce kitty treats were gone, and we at last did what had to be done.

My wife keeps two snapshots of Suzie in the frame of our bedroom mirror: One shows her sitting wide-eyed in the milk house of the old farm in the hand washing basin where she always kept my wife company as she did the chores. The other shows her sitting on the back patio railing, anxiously waiting to come inside and help me with my morning coffee. We still miss her so, so much.

Every once in a while, as I stumble from the bedroom to the kitchen in the early-morning twilight to plug my coffeepot in, I don't know why, but I'll occasionally stop and look for Suzie on the back patio railing.

Of course, all I ever see is our beautiful Finger Lakes cornfields and pastures. And darkness. As I sit here now at my desk, writing these stories, I look over at the empty armrest where she always sat, and I can almost see her there, her little head tilted, checking me out to make sure I do good.

I hope she likes what she sees.

CHAPTER EIGHT

LUCY

As they entered the exam room, the husband, beaming with excitement, spoke first. He had a smile as big as Texas.

"Hey Doc, how you doing? We got ourselves a new little kitten."

Sure enough, on the exam table in front of me now, purring like a motorboat, was a little longhaired ball of black and white fur that was one of the tiniest kittens I'd ever seen. She couldn't have weighed more than two pounds. I asked them where they got the little girl, and the wife said they'd just picked her up at an auction sale they'd been to over the weekend. I asked them her name, and they said it was going to be Lucy.

What a little sweetheart Lucy turned out to be. After this initial visit she came back in a couple more times for her booster shots and rabies vaccination. Each time they brought her back, she just kept getting mellower and mellower. She would just lie there as I examined her and gave her the injections. I had a little difficulty, however, in getting a good listen to her heart; she purred so much, I couldn't hear a thing.

And every time I was finished and reached down to give her one last pet, she'd always stand up and arch her back and stick up her tail and let me know just how much she appreciated the attention. She was a great little cat.

Soon it came time to get little Lucy spayed so that she wouldn't add to the surplus kitten population. The owners dropped her off the night before her big day, and like all parents, they were anxious about leaving their baby all alone in the cage. I assured them that all would go well.

Early the next morning, I put Lucy up on the examining table, listened again—with great difficulty (purr, purr, purr)—to her heart, determined she was OK, and then gave her the needle that would put her under anesthesia. When she was under, I placed her on her back on the surgery table. I then clipped and shaved the thick black hair from her belly in the area where I had to do surgery, cleaned and prepped the area down with antiseptic solutions, got myself scrubbed and gloved, and started the surgery.

When I got inside her belly, I discovered right away I had a problem. I couldn't find Lucy's uterus or ovaries.

Before I go on any further, I think a quick description of the spaying surgery is in order. When your veterinarian spays a cat or dog, what they are actually doing is performing open abdominal surgery to remove the female's reproductive organs: the ovaries and uterus.

The ovaries are the internal organs responsible for developing and releasing the female's eggs, and the uterus is the organ in which the developing fetus lives and grows.

During a routine spaying surgery, we veterinarians make an incision in the skin of the abdomen between the animal's belly button and pelvis. We then gently cut our way into the actual belly at which time all the animal's guts can be seen.

Then we take a special instrument with which we hook the uterus upward to the cut we just made. This allows us to get hold of both ovaries so that we can clamp them, tie them off, and then remove them.

Next, we clamp and tie off the uterus and remove it as well. After the removal of these organs, we sew shut all of the body layers we have just cut through and then wake the patient back up.

When everything goes as it should, the spay surgery is no big deal. The surgeon makes a nice, neat, small hole, and then gets in, does the surgery, and sews shut the hole. But in Lucy's case, I couldn't find the uterus. What this means is that I now had to make the entrance hole larger so I could see into more of her abdomen. I did that and still couldn't find poor Lucy's uterus.

"Damn," I said to myself, "What the heck is going on here?"

Since it wasn't possible for me to answer my own question, I fell back on the first rule of medicine, expressed by Hippocrates himself three thousand years ago: First, do no harm.

I would just tell the nice people that Lucy didn't have—or I just couldn't find—any reproductive organs. So I put all of Lucy's innards back where they belonged and stitched her back up. As I rolled her over from lying on her back to lying on her side, I noticed a slight swelling under her tail and rear end. With the fingers of my right hand, I parted her thick fur, and there, I made a profound discovery: There were two of the smallest testicles I'd ever seen.

Sweet little Lucy was a boy.

Because Lucy's parents both worked, I wasn't able to get hold of them to tell them the news until they came back later that night to pick him up. While trying my best to hide my embarrassment, I showed them, as Lucy just purred and purred away in front of us on the exam table, the larger-than-normal incision I'd had to make and related to them all of the details of the Lucy's long and difficult surgery.

After the rather lengthy explanation, I looked at them, they looked at each other, and then we all looked down at Lucy.

With great concern obviously showing on her face, the wife looked back at me and asked, "So what's all this mean, Doc?"

As straight faced and as seriously as I could, I said, "What this means is that your sweet little Lucy is a boy."

There was a moment of deep silence; even Lucy's purring stopped. Her owners looked at each other and a smile broke out on both their faces. They looked down at Lucy, and then looked at me and started laughing.

"Ain't that something," said the husband, smiling ear to ear. And Lucy went home and did just fine.

Some weeks later, I made the mistake of telling my former veterinary colleagues where I'd had my first job of my difficult surgery with Lucy; I never heard the end of it. For the next couple of years, every time I went to a medical conference, I was jokingly asked to explain my new method of neutering. They even sent me an impressive plaque for my office wall distinguishing me as an expert in spaying tomcats.

Over the next few years, I'd see Lucy for his annual vaccinations and worming or I'd see his owners with one of their other pets and always ask how my buddy was doing. The couple had decided that even though he was a boy kitty, he seemed to prefer the name Lucy, so they never bothered to change it. And Lucy grew into quite a substantially large cat. When they'd bring him in, he'd always lie on the exam table, just as calm as can be, looking like a huge black and white purring carpet.

One day, however, Lucy stopped eating. No matter what his owners did, he just would not eat. Not finding any obvious problem on examining Lucy, the first thing I did was take a blood sample from him and send it to the laboratory for analysis.

The results came back showing that Lucy's kidneys were failing. I told the owners that kidney disease is rare in young cats, and I had no idea why Lucy caught it. Although I gave Lucy's owners a poor prognosis, they wanted me to try to reverse the problem with hospitalization.

For the next five days I supported Lucy's body with fluids that we'd give through a catheter in his foreleg. Most cats hate this procedure and they bite, fight, claw, and generally act like wild beasts, but not Lucy. He'd just lie there like an angel and let the life-giving fluids flow into his veins.

Every day his mommy and daddy would come in to see him. One of the most amazing traits about Lucy was that no matter how sick he was, he'd just purr and purr and purr. And, believe it or not, he actually got better. On about the fifth day of therapy, he started eating, his color came back, and so I disconnected his fluids. By the next day he was eating and acting well enough to go home.

I told the owners, quite frankly, that I had no idea what was going on, and we'd have to take his recovery day by day.

All went well for about another year until one day, again, Lucy stopped eating. This time, however, his blood work came back a little worse. So I gave his owners another poor prognosis and then started the same medical therapy as I had before. The tough old fighter astonished us all and again turned around, so I sent him home.

But this time, the therapy lasted for only two weeks. We, both the owners and I, sort of knew that sweet little Lucy wasn't gonna make it this time. Although still purring, you could see in his eyes he just couldn't fight anymore. His disease was getting the best of him, and nothing I did could stop it.

I again catheterized him and hooked him up to fluids in an attempt to try to pull it off one more time. But by the second day, we all knew it was hopeless. With my blessings, his kind and loving owners made the difficult decision to put Lucy to sleep.

I brought him down from the hospital ward and placed him onto the exam table where I'd first met him years before as a tiny, purring ball of long black and white fur; where he had sat patiently as I told his owners about her turning out to be a him (I almost think on that day he was laughing right along with us); where he always lay like a big, hairy, carpet, responding passionately to caresses I gave him during his annual wellness exams; and where now he lay nearly in a coma.

With his mommy and daddy there to hold him, I took the cap off of the catheter I'd left in his leg and attached the syringe full of euthanasia solution. "Good-bye dear friend," I said (to myself) and gave him the injection that would end his suffering. In a couple of seconds, his purring stopped.

CHAPTER NINE

MACK

As I entered the exam room to see what I hoped would be my last patient of a long and difficult Saturday's afternoon office hours, the first thing I noticed was that the whole family was there: mother, father, and their three kids, all smiling and delighted to be at the vet's. And sitting on the exam table, wagging his tail to beat the band, was Mack, their little black Scottie.

"How you doing, Doc?" said Dad. "Good to see you again. Nothing too serious for you today, Doc. Mack is just here for his shots."

Worn out as I was, I couldn't help but smile right along with this beautiful family and their happy little dog. It was always a delight to see them. But I was also looking forward to Mack's uncomplicated and, hopefully, quick and easy office visit, because up until now, it had been one of those kinds of days: everything from an early-morning emergency for a beagle that got hit by a car to a gruesome big chow dog/little poodle fight.

I really needed a simple one, but it was not going to be. Mack's examination would turn out to be one of my worst nightmares come true.

I'd known Mack and his family since he was a little eight-week-old puppy. I remembered how thrilled the children were as they and their father brought in the new puppy for a checkup before they'd even taken him home from the pet store. It was going to be a surprise Christmas present for their mother.

I recalled how he winced and yipped as I gave him his first vaccinations. I remembered the kids' look of joyous relief as I gave Mack a clean bill of health. Thereafter, every time the dog was brought in for his annual shots, the kids would hold their ears and close their eyes like it was they who were getting the needles. But Mack never again yipped or barked as I gave him his shots; he was the perfect patient, and they were the perfect owners.

I started my examination of Mack with a quick look into his mouth. At a quick glance, all I noticed was that he was developing a little tartar buildup on his fangs and upper molars; this is not uncommon in a middle-aged dog. After a quick peek in his ears, I wrapped my hands around his neck and then slid them down under and behind the lower jaw. It was here that I got my first indication that something was wrong. Mack's mandibular lymph nodes were abnormally large.

The mother (because mothers always notice these things), sensing my hesitation and the extra attention I was paying the swollen glands, asked if everything was all right. I did my best to mask my concern as I pulled my examination flashlight from the drawer in front of me.

"I'd like to get a little closer look at his teeth," I said as I again opened Mack's mouth. "The lymph nodes in his neck are quite swollen. My hope is that it's just because of an infected molar I may not have noticed on my first look."

But Mack's teeth, other than the tartar buildup, were just fine, so I continued my examination of Mack's neck. After rechecking the glands in his neck, I continued sliding my hands down to the regions just in front of his shoulder blades. Much to my dismay, his prescapular lymph glands were also enlarged.

I looked up and saw ten anxious eyes fixed upon my every move. I said nothing. There was still the possibility that these glands were enlarged because of an infection in the head. Continuing my exam, I circled my fingers under Mack's armpits.

As I did, my heart fell to the floor; the axillary lymph nodes in his armpits were five times the size they should be.

"Ah poop (that's not the exact word I used)," I whispered to myself. "How am I gonna tell these nice people?"

My mind was a chaos of thoughts, feelings, worries, and dread. Despite my attempt at maintaining an objective smile, I'm afraid my silence gave me away.

"Doctor," anxiously asked the father, "is there something wrong?"

Not knowing quite what to say, I said nothing and, robot like, continued my exam, knowing now exactly what I would find. It took me about another five seconds to finish.

The inguinal lymph nodes on the inside of Mack's legs were swollen as were the popliteal nodes between the cheek muscles of his butt. The most likely cause of this lymphadenopathy (the word is the medical term for having every lymph node in the body swollen) was cancer.

Still not sure how I would break the terrible news to Mack's family, I forced a smile, opened the exam room door, and asked my wife, who was doing paperwork at the front desk, to step into the room.

"Hey kids," I said, "we've got this huge white rabbit out back in the hospital. Do you want to go back and look at it?" I detected a slight reluctance in their responses, but their curiosity got the best of them, and they left with my wife.

Alone now in the exam room with the parents and Mack, I told them of my findings of whole-body lymph node enlargement. I showed them and watched as they both felt for themselves all of Mack's swollen nodes. I mentioned the most likely cause was that most dreadful of words, cancer. We talked about the slim possibility of the enlargement being the result of a whole-body infection, about antibiotic therapy, biopsing and lab testing, chemotherapy, and of the possible successes or failures of the various treatments.

As the three of us stood there looking at sweet little Mack standing on the table in front of us, tongue out panting, happy as a clam, wagging his tail, and looking like he had not a problem in the world, the father asked, "Doc, if it's cancer, how long do you think he's got?"

This is a question I always dread having to answer. From experience, I knew it wouldn't be long, because, as far as cancers go, Mack's was a bad one. But people want an answer, and so with great trepidation I said, "If we're lucky, about two months."

I could tell from their silence that this was shorter than they had expected. As I was telling them what to look for as far as knowing when and how to tell if Mack was suffering or not, the kids came back into the exam room all excited and babbling about seeing the big rabbit out back.

The mother and father, on my suggestion, decided to take Mack home to live out his life. They would tell the children when they felt the time was right. I dispensed an antibiotic for Mack on the outside chance that his problem was just a massive infection and was relieved that they were the last clients for the day.

I thought about Mack afterward only occasionally. Many joys and the occasional tragedy had replaced the memory of his visit in my mind. My hope, as is my hope in all cases like this, was that I was wrong; maybe he just had a massive whole-body infection that caused his lymph nodes to react and maybe, just maybe, he'd gotten better.

However, as is always the case in these sorts of things, on a bright sunny day about three months later, the father, all by himself, brought the family's little buddy in for his last visit.

According to Dad, Mack kept up his appetite and cheerful disposition right up until the day before. At that time, he just lay down and no longer had the strength to get up. He could still manage a weak tail wag but was otherwise fading fast. He'd fought the good fight, but the cancer had won.

I asked the father if he wanted to be with Mack when I gave him the shot, and he said yes. I then got out the bottle of the blue liquid, and together, we sent Mack home.

Chapter Ten

Copper

"OK," I said, "bring my little buddy in, and we'll see what we can do to help him." And so began my short quest to save Copper's life.

Copper was a six-month-old short haired male tabby cat who I'd first seen as an eight-week-old kitten. One of the reasons he stuck out so profoundly in my mind among all of the other thousands of cats that I see was that he bore a striking resemblance to one of my and my wife's favorite former cats named Suzie.

He was such a well-behaved little guy, too, and so curious. I remember on that first visit how he just sat there quietly and attentively as I spoke with his owner. He would look back and forth between me and his daddy, occasionally cocking his head one way or the other as if he were actually listening. He did get a little feisty, however, as I gave him his injections (they all do). I saw him again about a month later for his second round of shots and then again at five months of age for his neutering surgery.

All went well until a couple of weeks later. During the evening office hours, Copper's family brought him in to see me because he'd been vomiting and not eating for two days. On physical examination I could find nothing significant: His color was good, his temperature was normal, and he was not at all dehydrated. The only possible problem might have been that he was seen eating an ornamental fern in a freshly cut flower arrangement the owner had received earlier in the week. His daddy noted he had seen pieces of the plant in his vomit.

Since it was Friday evening and no laboratory would be open for us to do blood testing, Copper's owners opted for conservative therapy. That is, we would treat the kitten with antibiotics over the weekend and then would reevaluate his response to this therapy at the beginning of the week. However, by the time Monday rolled around, his situation had deteriorated terribly. Copper was now on my exam table, dying right before my very eyes.

Again, I could find absolutely nothing wrong on physical exam except that Copper's body temperature was five degrees below normal. This was not good. My experience in this business has shown me that whenever an animal's temperature is so far below normal, they almost never make it. Although the situation seemed quite grim, Copper's daddy still wanted to go ahead and try to save him.

Since I had no idea what was going on, I decided to pursue the possibility that Copper had indeed poisoned himself by eating the fern from the flower arrangement. I checked with the florist who delivered the flowers, and he readily identified the fern and told me it was not poisonous to his knowledge. I then looked it up in my poisonous plant manuals and confirmed it was not a listed toxin.

Still not convinced that the plant wasn't to blame (there was really nothing else for me to go on), I drew some blood in order to perform some laboratory tests. I also placed an intravenous catheter into the vein of Copper's foreleg so that I could give him fluids and electrolytes to counteract his dehydration. The next day the blood test came back and showed that he was in kidney failure. His kidneys had shut down completely. Our only chance now was to continue with the fluid therapy we'd already started him on in the hope that his kidneys would be stimulated to start back up.

But as time went on, I could see in his eyes that we were losing the battle; he just kept slipping further and further. His kidneys were so bad that even with all of the fluids I'd given him over the previous two days, he had not produced one drop of urine. The poisons and toxic wastes that normal kidneys routinely remove just kept building up and building up in his system so that after three days, he was in a coma.

I called his owners and told them of Copper's condition. I mentioned he wasn't responding at all to anything, anymore, and was, for all intents and purposes, not too far from death. After a long discussion over the phone, the decision was made to put him to sleep; I was to wait, however, until his daddy could be with him and comfort him on his last journey.

When his owner arrived, I took him out back into my hospital where I had Copper bedded down in a large cage. He was lying there quietly on his side, completely incoherent, with just an occasional twitch or spasm to show he was still alive. I opened the cage door, and his daddy knelt down and softly called his name.

"Copper, hey little buddy, can you hear me?"

I broke the solemnness of the moment by reminding Copper's daddy that his little kitten was in a coma and he probably couldn't hear anything.

But the owner paid no attention and kept talking to him anyway. When nothing happened, he reached down to stroke the little cat's muzzle and cheek with his finger. And then, the most amazing thing happened. If I hadn't seen it with my very own eyes, I would never have believed it.

As his daddy was sounding his name for what would probably be the last time, Copper, without lifting his head or moving his eyes, slowly raised his tiny front paw, reached out, and laid it upon his owner's finger. The two of them then held this loving touch for what seemed an eternity.

When Copper was finished, he let his paw softly slip back down to the floor of the cage. Although I try to be quite detached and professionally objective at these moments, I have to admit that I was truly touched by the miracle I'd just witnessed.

Copper's owner stood up, and as he was saying his last good-bye to his little friend, I walked over to the drug cabinet, unlocked it, and filled a small syringe with the deadly euthanasia fluid. When I walked back over to Copper's cage, I discovered immediately that it was no longer needed. Copper had passed away. I guess he just wanted to hold on long enough to say good-bye to his daddy.

CHAPTER ELEVEN

CHARLIE

It was quarter past midnight when the phone rang. Not quite sure what was happening or, for that matter, even where I was, I rolled over and fumbled around in the darkness for the phone sitting on the nightstand. After about four rings, I located the receiver, picked it up, and mumbled, "Hello, Dr. Orzeck here."

"Doc, this is Charlie. Mama is trying to have her kittens."

Still trying to figure out what was going on, I asked, "How long has she been in labor?"

"She's just started. She's laying on her side heaving and meowing, trying to get them out. Doc, is she gonna be all right?"

"Charlie," I said, "if she's just started, we need to give her a little more time. Like I told you last week, nature figured this birthing stuff out a long time ago."

After making sure he calmed down, I gave him a couple of specific recommendations and told him I'd call him as soon as I got up at five o'clock.

My friend and client Charlie is quite a character. If you saw him and didn't know who he was, you'd probably be a little afraid of him, especially if he was decked out in his in his biker's leathers and tooling down the road on his Harley-Davidson motorcycle. But Charlie's looks are deceiving, because he is one of the gentlest and kindest men I know. And he loves his cats.

Mama, the subject of this early morning call, was a longhaired, tortoiseshell, nearly adult, kitty who just showed up one rainy and freezing late-autumn afternoon on Charlie's back porch.

The first thing Charlie did was bring her in for me to examine. He asked me if I knew anyone who'd lost a cat like this, and I told him I didn't. He then asked if I knew someone who wanted a cat, and I told him it was nearly impossible to get rid of a newborn kitten much less a nearly full-grown cat.

When I told him this, I could tell by his smile that he was happy with my answers and about a half second later he said, "Good, Doc, we'll (meaning he and his wife) just keep her then."

So I checked Mama (her name wasn't Mama yet) all over. She was in pretty rough shape. She was very malnourished, was suffering from exposure, and was infested with fleas. I gave her her first set of vaccinations, wormed her, and gave Charlie a fifty/fifty chance of her being able to pull through her malnourished condition if he could make sure she got good nursing care.

"No problem, Doc," Charlie said as he cradled the poor little kitty like an infant in his arms, "I'll take good care of her."

I knew he meant it.

About a month later, he brought her back for her booster vaccinations and another worming. I told Charlie—his wife was with him also this time—that he was doing a wonderful job with the cat and reminded him that in about two more months she'd be ready for spaying. He said he'd call for an appointment. But we both forgot, and that's the reason why we were talking to each other past midnight on that cold April evening.

Later that morning, as soon as I got up (after first putting on the coffee pot), I phoned Charlie to find out how his cat was doing. As I dialed the number, I was confident the whole thing would be over and that Mama and her kittens were doing just fine.

He answered the phone on the first ring. "She's quieted down some, but she's not had one kitten yet."

I told him to bring her into the office.

On the physical exam, I could find nothing wrong. She didn't appear to be having labor contractions, and she was not yet dilated. I told Charlie to take her back home and give her more time. I called him around noon and still nothing. He called at around four in the afternoon and said the cat was having contractions. I called him again at six, and he said there was nothing yet. I told Charlie to bring Mama back in.

This time she was indeed in labor, very violent labor. Mama was really hurting.

On examination, I discovered that even though she was having contractions, she was not dilated and therefore could not possibly get her kittens out. I told Charlie and his wife that our best bet would be to remove the kittens by caesarian section.

I told them that since I had to concentrate on the surgery and medical needs of Mama, my wife might need some help tending to the newborns as I took them out of the cat's uterus. If there were a lot of kittens, it would sure be handy if he could stick around and help.

He looked at his wife, she nodded back, and he said, "No problem, Doc, we'll do what we gotta do to help Mama and her babies."

Doing a C-section on a cat is not too big a challenge if everything goes smoothly. While I put Mama under anesthesia and prepped her for surgery, my wife, Charlie's wife, and Charlie got the towels, hot water bottles, boxes, and everything else they would need for the kittens. As I was scrubbing up and making the last preparations for surgery, I reminded Charlie once again that my only concern during the operation was going to be for Mama. Theresa and he would be in charge of the kittens.

"OK, Doc," he said with a serious conviction. "You do what you gotta do, we'll take care of things here."

So I gloved and gowned up and started the C-section surgery. As soon as I made the first incision and opened the cat's belly, I knew I had a serious problem. There was blood and uterine fluid and placental membranes all over the inside of the abdomen. Mama's uterus had ruptured, and there were two dead kittens floating among Mama's intestines. What a mess! I did discover, to my amazement, that there were two more kittens still in the uterus and still alive. So, I fast as I could, I cut into the uterus, incised their fluid sacs, and handed each of the slimy, slippery, precious babies, one by one, to my wife.

As she and Charlie and his wife struggled to keep the two infants alive, I assessed Mama's condition. It really looked bad. Before they died from lack of oxygen and nutrition that normally would have been provided by their mother's uterus, the two kittens I still had to remove had scratched and clawed many of Mama's guts and organs.

Everywhere I looked there were inflamed and bleeding body parts. After removing the dead kittens, I told Charlie what I'd found and that it didn't look too good for Mama.

As he cradled one of the newborns close to his body to keep it warm, he said, "Do what ya can, Doc. We got it under control here."

I removed the shattered uterus, did a quick spay, removed all of the floating parts I could find, flushed out all the blood and debris I could, and closed Mama back up. She was on her own now; time would tell. I cleaned the iodine prep solution from her belly and nipples and put her in a warmed-up box that Theresa had prepared for her still-alive kittens.

I gave Charlie and his wife a guarded prognosis for Mama (guarded is a nice way of saying I wasn't sure she was gonna make it), Theresa gave them some instructions on rearing the kittens, and we sent them all home with directions to call if Mama didn't come around. I also wanted to see her tomorrow to start watching for what I expected to be serious— and very likely, fatal—complications.

But Mama proved to be one tough cat. When I called Charlie the next morning, he said she had recovered from the anesthesia just fine, and she was now nursing and mothering her two new adorable kittens just like nothing had ever happened.

I could tell over the phone that Charlie was just beaming with pride. When later that week they brought the family in for a recheck, I told Charlie and his wife that although Mama was sill a long way from being out of the woods as far as complications were concerned, she looked real good so far.

A couple of weeks later, when they brought Mama and her little kittens back for me to remove her C-section stitches, I was absolutely amazed at how good the cat was doing. It really was as if nothing had happened.

Likewise, it was touching to see how taken Charlie was by the two little additions to his family. He could not have been a finer daddy. Over the next several months, I saw the little guys a couple more times for their vaccinations and wormings. They grew up to be a couple of little sweethearts who just plain loved their daddy.

I mean, when he brought them in, they'd crawl all over him and cuff and lick at his fingers, and purr like little airplanes when he picked them up. It was a precious sight to watch them all.

Winter came and went and as April rolled around, I'd kinda forgotten all about Charlie and his family of cats. But one afternoon, right in the middle of office hours, Charlie called to tell me that Mama had just crawled back home and that her hind leg was dragging behind her, bleeding real bad; he felt she'd been kicked by the neighbor's horse. Maybe she was hit by a car; he just didn't know.

When he brought Mama in about twenty minutes later, I X-rayed her and discovered that her upper leg bone was shattered into more pieces than I could count. Because of the severity of the fracture and the associated damage to the surrounding tissues, I felt that even in the hands of an orthopedic surgeon, there was just too much destruction. I told him it was my opinion that there was no alternative but to amputate the leg.

Charlie, big guy that he was, was absolutely devastated. But I calmed him down and he said OK. I assured him that if Mama survived the surgery, she would do just fine on three legs. I sent him home, finished up the afternoon's office hours, and got Mama ready, again, for surgery.

In veterinary college, the surgery instructors teach us students very specifically how to perform the operations we'll all need to survive as full-fledged vets; and they make it look so simple: You cut this tendon away from this bone, cut this muscle here, tie off this artery there. Just as neat as a pin until you start working on an actual accident victim like Mama.

All there was left was shattered, splintered bone and flesh that looked more like hamburger than muscle; there was absolutely not one normal structure left intact that I could have worked with.

So what do you do if you're the surgeon? Well, you just start sewing up what you can with what you got left. Then you close the hole and hope for the best. That's all I could do with dear Mama.

But as difficult as Mama's surgery was to perform, she did just great. The next day, she was even using the litter box. The cat was absolutely unbelievable. We kept her for another day to monitor her for infection, but there was no problem, and so I sent her home.

Two weeks later, Charlie brought her back in for her stitches to be removed and spent ten minutes telling me how Mama was back to catching mice and doing all of her all her old tricks, and best of all, she was more loving than she'd ever been. Her kittens (big kittens now) didn't recognize her at first, but after awhile they all settled back down.

All went well after that and, again, I sort of forgot all about my buddy Charlie and his cats. Then, on a hot summer afternoon I got a frantic call from Charlie; he was crying. "Doc, one of the cats just got chewed up by the neighbor's dog."

"Get her in here Charlie, as fast as you can!" I said as we both hung up. As I waited for Charlie to arrive, it dawned on me that he didn't say which cat it was. My thoughts went first to Mama, knowing her bad luck.

Ten minutes later, Charlie came barreling into the office and placed a blood-soaked T-shirt bundle on the exam table. As I gently unwrapped the carnage lying before me, my heart sank as I discovered it was one of precious kittens that we'd worked so hard to save the previous winter.

He was already gone. No one on this earth could have saved the little guy. Looking up from the lifeless body, I saw in Charlie's face a look of utter disbelief. I asked him, "You OK, Charlie?"

A couple of seconds passed by, and I asked again, "Charlie, you gonna be all right?"

"I should have seen it coming. That damn rottweiler is always in my yard," was all he said.

Another couple of seconds went by before I again broke the silence.

"You gonna call the sheriff, Charlie, and have them pick this dog up?"

I didn't tell Charlie at the time, but I knew from another neighbor that the dog had killed before, and I was hoping Charlie would make the call.

"No, Doc," he said as he picked up and cradled the dead kitten in his arms, "I'll take care of it myself."

And, as rumor has it, he did.

Chapter Twelve

Chief

When my wife handed me Molly's reminder card and asked what she should do with it, I answered that I wasn't quite sure.

I remembered that the Chief (Molly's owner) had called me about six months back to tell me he could no longer take care of himself all that well anymore; he and Molly would be moving in with his daughter's family in another state. I recalled the heartbreak and anguish in his voice as we said good-bye for what would be the last time.

After a couple of minutes during which I reminisced about my old friend, I told Theresa to go ahead and mail it; Molly and the Chief might just still be hanging in there.

I recalled with great fondness our first meeting.

"Wow, Doc, I think you're the only vet she's ever liked," said the old Chief as I was giving his little dog her distemper shot. "At the most, every other place I've ever been, all she seems to want to do is bite the doctor's face off. I think she likes you, Doc; I'm sure you and her will get along just fine."

And that's how I came to know the old Navy chief and his little (also old), sweet, shih tzu named Molly. Chief was a giant of a man who loved his little dog more than anything in the world.

We, the Chief and I, also got along real well. We realized instantly—because we saw the tattoos on each other's arms—that we shared the common bond of both having served in the U.S. Navy. After each visit, if the waiting room was empty, we'd talk at great length, as ex-sailors are apt to do, about our experiences.

Chief was severely burned on both his legs while serving as a young seaman aboard one of the battle-ships during the attack on Pearl Harbor. He was hospitalized (refitted was the way he put it), along with his ship, in California. After a long convales-cence, he rejoined another battleship just in time to be part of her crew as she provided protective naval bombardment for the D day troops landing on Normandy.

He said he spent just about his whole career on the battleships, but when the politicians mothballed the last one, he retired. He was quite the old salty dog, and I always enjoyed his visits.

Over the next few years, I saw quite a lot of the Chief and his little Molly. He was such a good daddy to her. Every time the dog had the smallest of coughs or went more than eight hours without eating, he'd rush her into the office.

"Doc, is she gonna be all right?" he'd ask with genuine, heartfelt concern.

During these emergency visits, this rugged man of the world, this scarred old warrior, would stand there nearly in tears as I examined his little Molly.

"Doc," he would plead, "please tell me she's gonna be all right; she's my only friend in the world."

It was always a very touching sight.

Molly's cough was usually easy to explain. I knew from her past history that she had a slight heart problem as well as a nasty reoccurring bronchitis that flared up every time the Chief fired up his woodstove. After throughly examining her just to make sure nothing else new had showed up, I would again remind the Chief that the ash and smoke from his woodstove was the most likely reason for her cough.

When he brought her in because she wasn't eating, careful inquiry would always reveal the fact that the Chief had most likely given her a piece (usually a very big piece!) of a pork chop he had prepared for himself the evening before. I'd look at him and tell him as firmly (of course with the utmost respect for his age and life experience) as possible, "Chief, Molly is getting old; the bottom line is that she can no longer tolerate any changes in her diet. I think she'll be all right this time, but you just can't feed her those fatty table scraps anymore."

And the Chief would just look at me and smile and then look toward his sweet little dog and tell me, "Ah Doc, when she looks at me with them big brown eyes, there's just no way I can tell her no."

Everything was going along great until one day the Chief brought Molly in because she was drinking bowl after bowl of water and not being able to hold her pee very well. We did blood work and a urine analysis on Molly and came up with the diagnosis of diabetes.

"Well, what do you know?" he exclaimed. "Ain't that something? I've had diabetes for years; I didn't know that dogs could get it. Do you think she'll need to get shots?"

I spent a while explaining how we were, indeed, going to give the dog shots and how we would then have to monitor her very closely. We set Molly up on an twice-a-day injection program (just like her daddy) and for a long time, she did quite well.

But both Molly and the Chief were aging before my very eyes, and each one's diabetes was starting to get the best of them. As time went along, the disease was getting so bad that the Chief could no longer drive because of his failing eyesight. Then the diabetes started affecting his legs. He went from needing a cane to having to use a walker and then finally, on his last couple of visits to my clinic, not being able to make it into my office at all; he'd just sit in the car and send Molly in with his neighbor friend.

After each exam, I'd always make a point of walking out to the parking lot to fill him in on how his little Molly was doing. The Chief looked tired, but he always had a story to tell me.

Sadly, his sweet little Molly wasn't doing too well, either. In due time, her blood sugar levels, despite the insulin injections, were still very high. She could hardly use her back legs anymore because of arthritis; she'd lost just about all of her teeth, probably as a side effect of her failing kidneys; and the same disease that eventually made her master blind had also robbed her of her eyesight. But just like her owner, she had a strong spirit and a fierce desire to live.

And so it was that a couple of months went by and I didn't see either the Chief or Molly. Then out of the blue, he called me to tell me his daughter was coming to pick him and Molly up, and she would be taking them both to live with her and her family down south somewhere.

He thanked me one last time for taking such good care of his little baby, I told him how honored I was to have known him, and then we said goodbye for the last time. The two of them would cross my mind every now and then, but I heard nothing more from him again. That is, until my wife sent Molly's reminder card.

The card, which I mailed to the Chief's old address, got efficiently forwarded to his daughter's home. Because he had gone on and on telling his daughter all about the good care I'd given his Molly, she felt that I would appreciate an update. I thanked her for her kindness, and she brought me up to date.

She told me that the complications of her father's diabetes had gotten the best of him, and he'd passed away about a month after he moved in with her. His little Molly was on his lap, as she had been every day since they had arrived at her home, when he finally sailed into that last sunset.

She told me how her father and Molly fought hard and gave their all to hang on and keep one another going. The day after he died, they took Molly to their local vet.

The daughter told me she looked just awful. She said that Molly just lay there on the doctor's table, not moving at all, except to gasp for air.

I could picture in my mind how her beautiful brown eyes—those same eyes that always softened her daddy into giving her pieces of pork chops—were now blind, swollen shut, and covered over with dried, crusty junk. My mind flashed back to the first day I saw her sitting there in her daddy's lap as he made out the check for the payment of her vet visit. I recalled how she just sat there, proud as a peacock, a little angel, and how every once in a while she would look up and lick her daddy's nose. I smiled at the memory.

The vet told Chief's daughter, correctly, that Molly was suffering and that putting her to sleep would be the most humane option. I told her that I probably would have recommended the same thing.

She told me her father was buried with full military honors and that Molly was with him, sitting on his lap forever in death as she had in life. As she told me this, I could again see little Molly in my mind's eye, sitting there, with tail wagging, her big brown eyes focused on the infinite horizon, guiding the old mariner forward, full speed ahead, as they sailed together, forever, on their final journey home.

I thanked her for calling, expressed my condolences on the loss of her father, and said good-bye.

CHAPTER THIRTEEN

BEN

Rabies is one of the oldest and most lethal diseases known to man and animals. It can be found in just about every country on earth. Control and prevention of this deadly disease is taken very seriously by governments and health workers everywhere because of its one absolute truth: Once you catch rabies, whether you're man or animal, you will die.

Although dogs and bats are the most common animals people think of when they think of rabies, the reality is that any warm-blooded animal, anywhere, at any age, can catch the disease. People tend to forget—or maybe they just don't know—that cats are especially prone to catching rabies. Excellent, highly effective vaccines are available for almost every species of animal imaginable, including humans.

Where I have my veterinary practice, starting in about 1991, an epidemic of raccoon rabies hit our area. Once it took hold, it spread rapidly into all of our other native species: dogs, cats, deer, skunks, cows, horses, and just about every other critter that walks.

One of the greatest challenges was getting people to vaccinate their animals. Despite enormous efforts by state health officials, radio and television personalities, and our local veterinarians, a great many people either never got the word or just plain chose to ignore the warnings to get their pets vaccinated. This indifference has resulted in some terrible consequences.

As I mentioned, health agencies don't mess around when it comes to rabies. In my state, one of the rules regarding the disease is that if any domestic animal (meaning all of our pets and farm animals) gets bitten or attacked by a wild animal but has an up-to-date rabies vaccination, all the pet owner has to do is reboost the pet's rabies shot. No problem.

Where we run into trouble is when a pet has been in an encounter with a wild animal and is not vaccinated. When this happens, there are one of two possible outcomes for the pet. The first is that if the wild critter who attacked the pet can be tested for rabies and the testing laboratory says the animal doesn't have the disease, then there's no problem.

However, if the wild animal is captured or killed and is found to be positive for rabies, or if the animal has gotten away and cannot be tested, then the unfortunate pet who was its victim has to be put to sleep. The reason for such a drastic measure is, of course, that the pet will probably come down with rabies, which will in turn put the pet owner's family at risk.

Although I've had to put to sleep many healthy animals, innocent animals whose only sin in life was their owner's negligence at getting them a rabies shot, I still hate doing it. I sort of rationalize to myself that it is for the good of humanity (and all that other junk), but it doesn't help much.

The worst part of the whole rotten deal is having to deal with the neglectful owners. And it's always the same whining and carrying on from the pissed-off owner who always has some lame—and I'm being very kind here—excuse for not having had their pet vaccinated.

Sometimes in their angry grief, they go so far as to place the blame on me. This I never, ever allow them to do. I tell these people firmly, in no uncertain terms, that unless they've been living on the planet Mars their whole lives, they must have known about rabies shots. I tell them that frankly, I don't want to hear it; this is their pet, their responsibility, and their fault. This direct scolding usually gets them angry, and I never see them again. But that's OK.

One of the most heartbreaking, most exasperating, and downright most senseless cases I've had to deal with in regards to this rabies problem had to do with a sweet, gentlemanly, eighteen-year-old cat named Ben.

Old Ben was brought into my office because earlier in the day, he'd been bitten by a raccoon. The case was kind of unusual in the sense that the owners actually saw the raccoon chase Old Ben across a beam in their horse barn and then bite him on the rear end.

The husband's father (who's a state game warden) happened to be there visiting for the afternoon, and so he ran to his pickup, where he kept a rifle, came back, and shot the raccoon dead. They then threw the raccoon into a garbage can and brought Old Ben into my office for me to treat his bite wounds.

When I examined Ben, I found that he did indeed have a minor bad bite wound to his right buttock. When his owners told me he was eighteen years old, I was surprised; he had the body of a much younger cat: nice shiny fur, sturdy and well-formed muscles, a strong and clear heartbeat, and just the nicest, sweetest personality. The wife went on to tell me how she'd gotten him as a kitten for her eleventh birthday, how he'd always been the perfect cat, and how she loved him so much.

When I told her the wound was no big deal and that it wouldn't even need stitching, she seemed very pleased. I went on to tell them that because he'd been in contact with a wild animal, all I had to do was just boost his rabies and then send him home with some antibiotics. He'd do just fine. As I reached into my cooler to pull out the vial of rabies vaccine, I suddenly became aware of an ominous silence.

It lasted for about a minute. She looked at her husband and then looked down at Old Ben. When she finally looked up at me, it was a look of absolute terror.

In near tears she cried, "Doctor, what do you mean by boosting his rabies? You're not gonna give him a shot! I don't want him to have any shots. He's never had a shot in his whole life."

I literally froze in my tracks. I could not believe what I had just heard. I stood there looking at this young couple, trying to figure out what in the heck was going on. Although this had been the first time I'd seen them as clients, they seemed well-educated. They were very articulate, spoke of owning a small horse farm, and were dressed well.

Finally, when I spoke, I looked the wife in the eye, the desperation, I'm sure, obvious in my voice, and pleaded, "Ma'am, tell me you're joking; please, tell me it ain't so."

She looked at her husband and then looked back at me and, with a mixture of defensiveness and concern, told me, "It's the truth, Doctor, I never liked getting shots myself, and so I never wanted Ben to get them either. I didn't want to put him through any pain."

"What about this rabies epidemic?" I asked. "What about the law that says all dogs and cats over three months of age have to be vaccinated?"

My exasperation may have been beginning to show. Becoming somewhat indignant, she said, "Doctor, I was well aware of the problem, but I decided not to pay any attention to it because he *never* goes outside."

At that moment, I wanted more than anything else in the world to ask her, "Lady, if this cat was strictly an indoor cat all his life, just how in the heck did he end up outside in your horse barn getting chased by a wild raccoon?"

But I didn't. Putting her on the spot like that would have been cruel and would not have served any purpose. So I just calmed myself down and held it all in. My flying off the handle would have accomplished nothing and would have only added to the heartbreak of what I now had to do.

I just stood there for about a minute without saying a word, trying to keep myself from exploding. I knew that I—or they—were now going to have to report Ben's injury to the health department authorities. I also knew what the health department was going to say. I looked at her; I looked at him; and I looked at Old Ben lying patiently like a big old couch potato on my exam table and could feel the rage growing inside me.

"Because your little Ben has been wounded by a wild animal, and because he does not have a valid rabies vaccination, we are going to have to notify the public health department," I said with as much objective detachment as I could. "That's the law."

Then, after waiting a couple of seconds for this all to sink in, I continued. "My preference is for you to make the call so that you can tell them why you never vaccinated the cat. Also, they'll have other questions concerning possible exposure to yourselves or your father-in-law."

Like every other time I've found myself in this situation, I noted, again, how the same response always plays itself out. The defensive indignation quickly gives way to deceptive denial.

"Doctor, I didn't know, blah, blah, blah; I thought that if I left him inside all of the time, he wouldn't need the shot; I thought he was too young or too old; I couldn't afford it, and on and on, one lame excuse after another."

After a couple of minutes of these sorts of excuses, the owner's denial will quickly turn into an anxious concern. "What about the danger to my kids, my other pets, ourselves? Are we all gonna have to get shots? Will we have to put our pet to sleep?"

Although I knew the answers to all of these questions, I told this young couple that they would have to call the health department for the precise answers. They're the ones who gets paid the big bucks to answer these questions. I kept to myself the knowledge that if they test the dead raccoon for rabies and it's positive for the disease, Old Ben's life is over;

because I didn't want to worry them unnecessarily, I didn't mention that if the health department determines any of them had any contact with the raccoon, then they'll have to get rabies shots themselves; finally, I kept to myself the possibility that if this couple has any other pets who came into contact with Ben, their lives may be over as well.

So the couple left my office with a mixture of anger toward me for pointing out their neglect and fear for what awaited them with regards to their own and their dear little Ben's health.

I got a call later that day from the health department saying they were going to test the raccoon and would then make a decision. They told me that the owners would not need shots because they didn't have any contact with the dead raccoon, but that Ben's only hope, because he was actually bitten, is if the raccoon tested negative for the disease. We all hoped for the best.

But the best was not to be. The next afternoon, the health department called me and informed me that the raccoon did indeed have rabies. Because Ben had been bitten and would very likely then come down with rabies himself because he was not vaccinated, they were ordering him destroyed.

The health officer and I talked for a couple of minutes about this case, both of us lamenting the senselessness of the whole thing; but this was the way it had to be. They said the owners would bring Ben in that evening.

I came into the office for evening clinic hours in a state of absolute dread; I didn't want to have to do it. My sincerest wish that evening was that I had angered the couple so much that they would take Old Ben to someone else. This, also, was not to be.

Just before closing, the husband brought him in. He told me that his wife just couldn't deal with having to do this. I looked at Old Ben lying magnificently on the table. He had lived for eighteen years and probably could have lived another five before dying of old age. I felt the anger rising back up inside me. I wanted, again, to lash out at his owners for their arrogance, cowardliness, neglectfulness, and whatever else I could think of.

But I didn't. It would accomplish nothing. I asked him if he understood why this had to happen. He told me he and his wife did. The nice lady at the health department told them that if Ben came down with rabies because of being bitten, he would then place himself and his family at grave risk.

I nodded an OK and looked down at Old Ben one last time as he lay there on my exam table. His only sin in the world was not having a rabies shot. I told him—to myself—just how much I hated to have to do this to him, gave him one last pet on his head, and then gave him his needle.

CHAPTER FOURTEEN

SAM

People sometimes forget that the practice of veterinary medicine is a business. Some people will argue that this should not be the case; that we veterinarians are different and we, therefore, should perform our humane mission of saving innocent animals and easing their suffering out of the kindness of our hearts.

The reality is we veterinarians are burdened by the same overhead that every business in the world has to deal with: enormous school loans, income taxes, mortgages on real estate, electric bills, drug bills, employee salary, and many other expenses.

Like all people who are in business, veterinarians must be constantly on the lookout for clients who, on purpose, are trying to rip us off by not paying their bill.

One of the most common techniques is, of course, to write bad checks. Some strategies, however, if they weren't so despicable, would deserve an Oscar for their creativity.

One of the most profound examples of that happening in my practice involved a lady who came in with her sick cat, a local minister, and two sobbing young children. I'd told her previously to this visit not to ever come back until she paid me what she already owed. But, as she sat in the waiting room pleading with me to treat her cat, the minister, who was looking me directly in the eye, kept reminding me of how precious the cat was to the little children, how lucky the community was to have a healer such as myself, and on and on.

I never had a chance. I treated the cat (it had a minor upper respiratory infection) and got stuck with another bill.

So with this and all of the other experiences with nonpaying deadbeats in mind, when Stanley stopped in and asked if he could pay me later after he got home, I had to make a decision. He'd just set his new yellow Lab puppy on the exam table in front of us, and before I could answer, he said, "Doc, I just wanna make sure he's OK before I take him home."

Before I had a chance to say a word, he added, "And could you give him his shots while he's here?"

I had to make a quick assessment.

Here was this young guy, probably in his early twenties, with shoulder-length brown hair, who was wearing a black leather jacket and looking like he'd just returned from a Grateful Dead concert. The voice of experience in my head told me that he'd be a risk. But my intuition told me something else, because when we shook hands during our introduction, his grip was strong and his hands were hard, so I knew he was a working man. And there was a sincerity in his voice and an honest look in his eye.

Without any more thought, I took a chance and said, "As long as you tell me you'll be back later, there'll be no problem."

I finished the exam and gave Stanley's new puppy a clean bill of health and his first shots. As he left Stanley said, "I'll be back later, Doc," and was gone.

My wife, who felt the same way I did about Stanley, told me not to worry, and I never gave it another thought during the rest of the afternoon office hours. Sure enough, about ten minutes before closing, Stanley stopped back, as he promised, and paid his bill. Since no one was in the office, I stopped for a while to chat with him. It turned out that he was a part-time musician and that he worked full-time with his three brothers and his father in their family's house painting business. He was a very bright kid, and I enjoyed our talk a lot.

I saw Stanley a few more times over the next couple of months (as well as his father, all three of his brothers, and his one sister) for his puppy's shots and neutering. Stanley and his pup, whose name was Sam, bonded extremely well, and you never saw them apart. All went along fine until one early spring day

Stanley brought Sam into the office as an emergency. The poor dog was limp in his arms and very near death. I asked what happened, and he said he didn't know. Sam had pinpoint pupils, had shallow breathing, and a weak pulse. As my wife and I were placing a catheter to get some fluids into him, I discovered the fact that the day before, he had gotten into and had eaten several of Stanley's mother's tulip and daffodil bulbs.

So we passed a stomach tube and flushed out what was left in his stomach and then gave him a large quantity of activated charcoal to absorb any of the excess poisons left in his guts. All we could do then was provide life support.

For three days, all Sam did was lie in his cage. And every day, his daddy would stop on his way home from work to visit. It was hit and miss for a while, but Sam eventually recovered without a hitch.

The reunion between Stanley and his dog was one of the most touching I'd ever seen; I was glad it turned out so well. Afterward, you never, ever saw Stanley without Sam. If I ran into him at the grocery store, Sam would be in the truck; if I saw him at the sandwich shop, old Sam would be tied up outside.

Then came the tragic day. I remember it was summer, early summer as a matter of fact, and I was just finishing up Saturday afternoon office hours. Through the front door burst Stanley, tears flowing down his face, carrying his limp and bleeding Sam. As I helped Stanley lay his dying friend on the exam table, I knew instantly the wounds were from a shotgun.

It turned out that Sam decided on this nice summer day to go over to the neighbor's farm and chase his chickens. Without a single warning, the neighbor blasted Sam and called Stanley on the phone to come over and get the dog out of his yard.

I set to work trying to figure out where to start. Sam had taken a direct hit from the shotgun blast right in his chest and abdomen. I felt that the damage to his lungs, guts, organs, and spinal cord were just too extensive for anyone to ever be able to fix, but I told Stanley I'd give it my best shot anyway.

After just a couple of seconds of thinking it over, Stanley sobbed, "Put him down, Doc. I don't want my buddy to suffer anymore."

I said OK and gave Sam the needle that would take away his pain and to put him to rest.

"Thanks, Doc," Stanley said as he picked up his fallen comrade. "I'm gonna take him home and bury him on the farm. I'll stop back later to pay ya."

And he did.

CHAPTER 15

FLOPSEY AND MOPSEY

It had been one of those long and slow, dead-of-the-winter, February days, and I was glad it was almost over. As much as I enjoy this business, I have to admit that I was glad this middle-aged couple, the last clients of this evening's office hours, were finally done and on their way out the door. I'd been nursing some kind of an upper respiratory flu bug for about a week and was run down, exhausted, and maybe even a little cranky; and they, seeing I was not at all well, insisted on not giving me even the slightest break: questions, questions, questions; and then the same questions, again and again.

And to top it all off, just as they stepped outside and were about to close the door, the wife turned around, poked her head back in, and said, "Now Doc, you take real good care of them; you know they're our babies."

For just a second, I thought about giving her a piece of my frazzled little mind, but I didn't. In what I felt was an Oscar-winning performance, I managed to force one last desperate, exasperated smile and then told her the same thing I tell everyone else who makes this comment to me: "Ma'am, I treat everyone's pet the best I possibly can."

She seemed happy with that answer and in another second was gone into the cold night.

The husband and wife had just dropped off Mopsey and Flopsey, two very nervous female cocker spaniels, for spaying surgery the next day. After completing the paperwork at the front desk, they brought the two dogs into my exam room where I then gave each one a physical exam to check for any obvious problems that might complicate their surgeries.

I could see right off that Flopsey was sort neutral toward both of her owners and was quite independent. Mopsey, on the other hand, was obviously Daddy's little girl; the whole time she was on the table, she never once stopped looking at or cuddling up next to the husband.

I declared both dogs to be in good health and then, like all doctors, whether for humans or animals, explained in great detail all of the dangers involved with general anesthesia and surgery. When I finished, I asked them both if there were any questions. That was probably a mistake because, as I already mentioned, they did have questions—about a million of them.

This having to give warnings about the dangers of surgery and anesthesia is always a difficult part of my interactions with clients, and it's something I never take lightly. The warnings seem to scare a lot of people. One of the reasons for this fear is because it seems that everyone in the world, at one time or another, has known a relative or friend who had gone under anesthesia, many times for just some simple operation, and who never woke up.

After a couple of seconds to ponder what I'd just said, they told me they understood the risk. We then all walked back to the kennel area, placed Mopsey and Flopsey into the same big cage, and after a very emotional good-bye, Mommy and Daddy left.

The next morning, I arrived bright and early at the clinic to get a good start on the day's surgeries. As I turned the lights on and walked into the kennel room, little Flopsey jumped right up and ran to the front of the cage to greet me. Mopsey also got up but sort of stayed shyly in the back of the cage.

Since she seemed the friendliest, I hooked the leash onto Flopsey's collar first and carried her outside to the front lawn of my clinic so she could do her business. After doing so, I took her back inside, gave her her anesthetic injection, and did her spay surgery. When I was finished, I laid her in the recovery cage and went back to the kennel to get Mopsey.

This time, Mopsey came right to the front of the cage to greet me without any problem. (She probably had to go to the bathroom really badly by now.) Just as I did with her sister, I put a leash on her and walked her out into the cold February morning to let her pee and poop. During our walk together, she pranced around like a queen with her cute bushy tail waving proudly in the air and kept jumping up on my leg, wanting some affection. I gave her some, but after a while, told her we had to get back inside and get started.

After rechecking her heart to assure myself nothing was wrong, I weighed her and gave her the injection of anesthesia solution, and watched her closely as she went under. When she finally was asleep, I placed her onto the surgery table and started preparing her belly for the surgery. As I was just about done, I paused for a second; something just wasn't right. In another split second, I came to a terrible realization: Mopsey had stopped breathing!

Worse yet, when I felt her chest, her heart had stopped also. Ah shoot! Every doctor's worst fear had just happened; Mopsey was having a reaction to the anesthesia injection and was now in cardiac arrest. Without a second of hesitation, I gave her some emergency drugs and started CPR procedures. For the next fifteen minutes, I pumped her chest and inflated her lungs, but it would be to no avail. Sweet little Mopsey, the precious and proud little dog that I'd walked and played with on the front lawn of my clinic just minutes before, was gone.

Exhausted and mentally devastated, I just stood there for an eternity, not knowing what to do next. I put my stethoscope to her chest in the hope of a miracle; but none would be forthcoming. I thought that maybe, just maybe if I waited long enough, I would wake up; that, possibly, by some miracle, this was all just a terrible dream.

But I wasn't dreaming; Mopsey was dead and I was going to have to deal with it. It was my problem. I had set into motion the forces that led to this moment, and now I had to live with the consequences.

First, I checked little Mopsey's mouth to see if perhaps she'd thrown up and then sucked some of the vomit down into her windpipe. This was not the case. So I placed the cause of this tragedy on the most likely possibility, an allergic reaction to the anesthetic drug. That done, I now had to deal with her parents, especially her loving and trusting daddy. Since it was my first solo loss (by solo I mean the responsibility was mine alone and nobody else's), I didn't quite know what to do.

I remembered as a student in my final year at vet school watching this happen to one of the senior residents with a cat he was doing surgery on. He was quite nervous about it but was lucky in the sense that he had the ability to spread the blame (if you can call it blame) among all of us who were assisting him. Also, the owner in that particular case didn't seem to take it too badly; his exact words were, "Doc, it's just a damn cat."

On my first job, I had the opportunity to watch one of the senior doctors at the practice break the news to two different clients in one day that their dogs had passed away while under anesthesia. The first lady took the news without much problem because it was her husband's hunting beagle, and she just didn't care all that much for the dog. The second lady, who was a little older, took it real hard. She flat out screamed, "Oh my God, my poor baby," then broke down and wept uncontrollably.

It was awful. I remember telling my associate that I sure hoped that never happened to me. I remember he looked at me, obviously still quite shaken, and said something about it happening to everyone; it would be just a matter of time.

Still not quite sure what to do, I called my former boss and told him all about it. He'd told me to call him if I ever got in a jam, and I was glad he was there for me. I told him I felt just awful, that I was scared, that I was questioning my ability, that I wanted to run away, that I just didn't know what to do.

He was very comforting. First of all, he reminded me that this stuff just happens, and that's just the way it is.

He then reminded me that in his forty years of doing veterinary medicine, the constant reality of anesthetic accidents still torments him and that he dreads, more than anything in the world, having to tell a pet owner the bad news. So, the only thing that I could do, he said, was face it head on, answer any questions they may have, and always tell the truth. He wished me luck, and we said good-bye.

I picked up the phone and dialed the number on the information sheet. The wife answered. I told her as carefully as I could that Mopsey had a reaction to the anesthesia, her heart had stopped, and she was dead. I then explained how I'd done all I could, but I just could not bring her back.

She said she understood and added she would call her husband at work and they'd be in later to pick up Flopsie. She added that she would talk it over with her husband about what they were going to do with Mopsey's remains; she thought he'd probably want to bury her at home. I said one last time that I was sorry for her loss, and we said good-bye. After I hung up the phone, I said to myself, "Gee Rich, that wasn't too bad."

But nothing in this world is ever simple. Five minutes later, the phone rang. It was the husband. Obviously very upset, he cried, "Tell me it's not true, please Doc, not my Mopsey."

With a terrible, wrenching knot in my stomach, I had to tell this gentle man that his little dog was gone, that I'd done all I could, and . . . .

I couldn't finish; all I heard was this dreadful wail and the click of the phone being hung up. I thought about what just happened, gathered my wits back about myself, and went on and finished my morning's work.

Later that evening, the wife came in to pick up Flopsey, who was just jumping around all over the place and glad to see her mommy. The husband did not come with her. I explained to her, again, everything I could think of regarding Mopsey's misfortune, and answered all of her questions. I carried the box containing Mopsey's body out to her car for her and noted with mixed feelings—mostly relief—that her husband was not there either.

As I walked back to the office, I stopped on my front porch for a minute to think about all that had transpired that day. The coward that lives inside of all of us at one time or another was still relieved I didn't have to deal with the grieving husband. It would have been just terrible.

But the real person, the professional veterinarian, the caring fellow human being in me wished I could explain to him, face-to-face, how I tried so, so hard to save his beloved little dog and how sorry I was about his loss. But I never had the chance. The wife waved, pulled away, and I never saw either of them again.

CHAPTER SIXTEEN

TOY

During her first lambing on our farm, Mama Dorset begat Hot Dog and Lambie Pie. Because Hot Dog was able to feed from her mother as nature intended, she grew up to be a healthy, happy sheep who, in turn, over the many years we had her, blessed us with many offspring. Lambie Pie, as we all know, didn't make it.

It was one of those cold, upstate New York, late-winter evenings. We'd just returned home from the day's milking chores and upon walking out to the sheep barn, discovered that Hot Dog had just moments before given birth to a single, enormous female lamb. Thinking she was all done giving birth, I picked up the newborn and placed her into a small nursing pen. Then, as I was lifting Hot Dog in order to put her in with her baby, I suddenly heard a strange plopping sound. This was followed a split second later by a frantic, gurgling baby lamb's baa. Hot Dog, without the slightest bit of warning, had just given birth to a second baby.

After quickly setting her back down, I reached down into the warm, steaming pile of birthing fluids and afterbirth and pulled out the struggling little infant. I called my wife over from where she had been filling up the water buckets, and we went to work to try to save this second lamb.

I was sure we were gonna lose him—he was so small. But the little guy had the heart of a tiger, and after a few gasps to clear his lungs of fluids that had nearly suffocated him, he started breathing normally. He was so tiny, he could stand on the palm of Theresa's hand; he looked just like a little stuffed toy. So that's what we named him, Toy.

Toy turned out to be quite a character. Because he was so small and couldn't quite reach Hot Dog's nipples, he had to be bottle-fed. And, as all livestock growers know, bottle babies always become pets.

So we had him castrated so he wouldn't be mating with any of his relatives, and he grew to be a normal-sized, healthy sheep. He also sort of took a special liking to me, which is unusual. Whenever he'd see me walk into the barn, he'd let out an excited baa and come running over to be petted and given a handful of grain.

If it was summer and he was out on the pasture, he'd always come over to see me and beg for a handful of fresh-picked grass or a taste of his favorite sweet feed. He was my little buddy.

But there was always one problem with Toy. In the sheep business, a neutered male sheep produces no income whatsoever, and they eat like crazy. So, when he was about two years old, something came over me, and I got the notion to become serious about sheep farming. I made up my mind to get rid of any nonproducers.

With a hardened heart, I loaded Toy on the truck and took him to a livestock auction. I unloaded him onto the dock, watched the auctioneer put a sales tag in his ear, walked away without turning back, and got into my truck.

As I started to drive away, for some reason, I happened to catch a glimpse of Toy as he was still standing there on the loading dock waiting his turn to be taken inside to the sales arena. Maybe it was my imagination, maybe it was just my guilty conscience, but I saw on the gentle face of my little friend the most frightened look I'd ever seen. I decided right then and there I couldn't leave him. I just couldn't leave my buddy standing there all alone.

So I parked my truck and walked back over to the loading dock. After enduring several minutes of good-natured taunting and abuse from all of the old-timers who regularly hang around all of these country auction barns, I then struck a deal with the auctioneer with regards to his lost commission, and I unconsigned Toy.

As I walked around the corner of the barn back to the loading dock where I'd left him just ten minutes before, I saw him still standing there, eyes still fixed in the direction he'd last seen me.

I hollered out, "Where's my boy Toy?" In a flash he turned around. The second he saw me, he let out an excited little baa and ran over to greet me. After a couple of seconds of telling him how sorry I was to have scared him so, I picked him up, carried him back to the truck, cut the sales tag from his ear, and brought him back home. With just a couple exceptions, he would never leave the farm again.

After that, for about the next sixteen years, my old buddy became what's known in the livestock business as a pasture ornament. Old Toy just lived the good life of a simple, happy sheep. When I had gotten into vet school, one of his favorite adventures was to come with me to the school's annual open house. Here we would sit together as thousands of people petted him and felt his soft and delicate wool. He was an absolute ham, and everyone just loved him.

My wife and I even figured out a way (at least in our own minds) to justify our keeping him on the farm. Because he'd been around so long and was wise to the ways of the sheep world, he was a calming influence on the rest of the flock. Until his last couple of years, at which time his arthritis started slowing him down, he would lead the flock every morning out to pasture and in the evening, he'd march everyone back to the safety of the barn. If some of the younger sheep happened to break through the fence, all we would have to do is let Toy loose, and he'd round them up.

As time went on, though, old Toy started showing his age. It got so that in his last year, he had only a couple of teeth left. This meant he couldn't graze the pasture as well as he needed to. In order to insure he got enough to eat, we therefore had to keep him supplied with hand-pulled grass and good quality cattle feed, which he absolutely loved.

However, even if his teeth had been good, the pain in his old, arthritic joints kept him from wandering too far from the barn. Despite these two limitations, all went along just fine. That is, until one day in early September.

My wife and I had just returned home from a very long day of work at my veterinary clinic, and the first thing we noticed was that Toy wasn't there to meet us. So we went out behind the barn and saw immediately that he had fallen over and was stuck upside down on his back in a small drainage ditch that ran through the pasture; the poor old guy was overheated from struggling to get right side up again and was in a near coma. He looked so bad that I had my wife run back down to the office to get my euthanasia fluid. I was sure I was going to have to put him to sleep.

While she was gone, I stayed out in the field with my old friend. With some effort, I managed to get him propped up onto his haunches. After getting him stabilized, I then began to perform physical therapy on his stiffened limbs. And to my utmost amazement, he started to respond. Within about five minutes, he was again able to stand. So I left him for a second and ran to the barn to get him a handful of his favorite sweet feed. Again, much to my surprise, he actually ate it.

By the time Theresa got back, Toy was almost his old self. As a matter of fact, the minute he saw her walking into the pasture, he welcomed her with a weak but beautiful baa of delight. But as I look back on that sunny September afternoon, I sometimes wonder if I'd really done the right thing; even though I saved him, he would never be the same. His poor old knees and elbows just kept getting worse.

I had the needle and syringe of euthanasia solution in my hand ready to go, but I just couldn't bring myself to do it. I could tell by the look on his face that he wasn't ready yet.

So we kept him propped up on a bale of hay at night, and during the day, as long as the green grass lasted in the yard, we would move him around so he could nibble away on the tender leaves. Every day I would give him pain medication for his arthritic joints, and my wife would give physical therapy to his old limbs.

One time, believe it or not, he had rallied so well that he was actually standing on his own one warm October evening, waiting for us to return home. He looked so proud of himself standing there in the yard; I know if he could have talked he would have gloriously cried out, "Hey there! My human friends, look at me!"

But it didn't last long. The arthritis in his joints soon put him back on the bale and there were days his appetite would fail him. I kept a syringe of euthanasia solution at the house just in case his time had come. For a veterinarian, especially when one of your own pets is involved, the ability to euthanize, to put to sleep, to end suffering, to end a life, can be an overwhelming and oppressive burden. The decision of when to put Toy down was one I grappled with all winter.

It seemed like every time I thought he couldn't go on, he'd look at me, speak his little low-pitched baa, and eat another handful of grain. I kept telling my wife when she brought up the subject of putting him to sleep the same thing I always tell my clients when they ask me about their own suffering pets: that he'll tell me when he's ready.

And one day in early March, he finally did.

As I pulled the empty syringe and needle from the vein of his now lifeless arm, his old tiger of a heart at long last stilled, I had a vision of him young and strong-limbed again, bounding along on the sweet by and by, grazing the green, grass pastures of eternity.

In the evening, I know as he lies down beside the still waters, that precious little Lambie Pie, little

Lacie, good old Mama Dorset, wide-eyed Suzie, Sam, Lucy, Copper and all of the rest, will forever be by his side.